Five Biblical
Portraits

Books by

ELIE WIESEL

Night
Dawn
The Accident
The Town beyond the Wall
The Gates of the Forest
The Jews of Silence
Legends of Our Time
A Beggar in Jerusalem
One Generation After
Souls on Fire
The Oath
Ani Maamin, a Cantata
Zalmen, or the Madness of God
Messengers of God
Four Hasidic Masters
A Jew Today
The Trial of God
The Testament

Five Biblical Portraits

Elie Wiesel

University of Notre Dame Press
Notre Dame • London

Library of Congress Cataloging in Publication Data

Wiesel, Elie, 1928–
  Five Biblical portraits.

  Bibliography: p.
  Contents: Joshua — Elijah — Saul — [etc.]
  1. Bible. O.T.–Biography. I. Title.
BS571.W547   221.9′22 [B]   81-40458
ISBN 0-268-00957-0   AACR2

Manufactured in the United States of America

For André Neher in Jerusalem
and
Robert McAfee Brown in California

Contents

Joshua

Vayehi aharei mot Moshe eved adoshem. "And
it came to pass that when God's servant Moses died,"
*vayomer adoshem el Yeoshoua ben Nun mesharet
Moshe leemor,* "God told Moses' aide Joshua, son of
Nun, as follows: 'Moses has passed away and you are
now his successor, you are now your nation's leader;
go and cross the river Jordan; go and occupy the land
which I have chosen for the children of Israel. Every
spot on which your foot treads I give to you, as I
promised Moses. Your territory shall extend from the
wilderness and Lebanon to the Great River Euphrates
—the whole Hittite country—and up to the Mediter-
ranean Sea. . . . No man shall be able to resist you as
long as you live. As I was with Moses, so I shall be
with you; I will not fail you or forsake you.' "

Thus begins the narrative of a stunning adventure, the echoes of which reverberate in our consciousness—and in our newspapers—to this day: a
nation still exuberant and young, still homeless, is
about to take possession of its territory, still inhabited
by other tribes and other entities, in the name of an

1

ancient promise, on the authority of a higher, inscrutable will.

This first chapter in the Book of Joshua serves as introduction to and prefiguration of all that will follow.

God, Moses, Joshua, Israel: four characters in a cast of multitudes, in a drama that is yet to be concluded, and never will be. Only their interplay may change. At times all four seem to be on the same side, but only at times. God is God and God is one—and He dominates the others, all the others, as well He should—but the other three occasionally dominate one another, or at least try.

Why the explicit distinction between Moses and Joshua? Why is Moses called *eved adoshem* and Joshua *mesharet Moshe? Eved* means servant, slave, serf, whereas *mesharet* means aide or assistant. One can be the *mesharet* of another person, to another person, but one can be the *eved* of God alone. We are all His servants. Why is Joshua defined by his relationship to Moses, not by his relationship to God? Also: why such emphasis throughout the chapter—and, indeed, throughout the entire Book of Joshua—on his association with Moses? The name Moses is mentioned eleven times in the first chapter alone—and fifty-three times in the book. Why?

While most good questions remain questions, this one is an exception and can be answered.

Remember: Moses has just passed away. Up in heaven, the angels and seraphim greet him with joy, welcoming him as a home-coming messenger who has accomplished a mission. Heaven glorifies him seven times, the waters glorify him seven times, the fire glorifies him seven times.

But down below, at the foot of Mount Nebo, in the desert, the orphaned children of Israel weep. And all of creation weeps. And in his sorrow, Joshua forgets three hundred commandments and acquires seven hundred doubts. The bereaved people, blinded by grief and perhaps by guilt too, want to tear Joshua to pieces for having succeeded his teacher Moses.

Clearly, the newly appointed young leader is thinking constantly of his illustrious predecessor. He is not sure of himself, of his own virtues and merits. Will he manage to meet God's expectations of him? Will he prove himself able to continue the work that only a Moses could begin? Will he be able to lead? And will the people obey? The two tasks were equally difficult: the first, to take the Jews out of Egypt; the second, to bring them into their promised land. It was as great a challenge to lead the first generation of free Jews as it had been to lead the last generation of Jewish slaves.

The admonition *Hazak veematz*, "be strong and courageous," is repeated three times in the very first chapter, twice by God and once by the people. Do they doubt Joshua's strength and courage? Even after Moses' death, he seems to remain his second-in-command. The disciple has not yet freed himself from his master. He feels incapable or perhaps unworthy of assuming his own destiny as leader.

And so God strengthens Joshua's self-assurance by promising him all that He ever promised Moses, and more. Moses has adversaries, even enemies—not

3

Joshua. *Lo yityatzev ish lefanekha*, says God, "No one will ever dispute your authority." What an advantage for a political leader—to rule without opposition, without intrigues and plots. Such an impossible gift could be given only by God. And since in Judaism nothing ever takes place without historical—and rhetorical—background, God reminds Joshua of His past pledges and covenants: "This land is yours, Joshua." And He goes as far as to indicate its boundaries. "All this is yours. You will be the one to fight Israel's great territorial wars; and you will win them."

Joshua: the fiercest warrior, the bravest commander in Jewish history, and its most victorious general as well. No wonder that his name figures in West Point's Hall of Fame as our civilization's first and foremost strategist and field commander.

But then, why was he torn by so many doubts? With God, history, and the people on his side, why was he so hesitant? He had been elected by God, appointed by Moses, cheered by the whole nation, and yet he was still uncertain of his own role. He needed to be told again and again *Hazak veematz*, "be strong and courageous," he who, by virtue of his office, should have given strength to others.

That he doubted himself in the beginning, there is no question. But what about later? Did he stop doubting? And if so, when? After which battle, which victory?

Joshua: there is an air of mystery about him. He was tragic and perhaps misunderstood in his glory, for his life was filled with dark, implacable violence in the service of God, whose name is—peace.

His biography is one long, exulting yet blood-chilling adventure, which raises vital questions about Judaism's attitude towards conquest and war. When is violence permitted, when even commanded? When is war justified? When is it a curse? Is it ever a blessing—if so, when? What is the link—is there a link—between Jewish geography and Jewish morality?

Joshua's concerns remain ours, his anguish is our anguish. May one go too far in order to assure one's survival? A living bridge between slavery and redemption, Joshua had to decide for himself, and for his nation, where the past ends and where the future begins, where vision and memory meet, and when they are in conflict.

No adventure is as exciting, as stimulating, as full of promise and fire. His name evokes Shiloh, Hebron, Jericho—and so many other biblical names that have recently re-entered international diplomacy. Who may settle in Hebron: Jews or non-Jews? Joshua must have spent sleepless nights over the West Bank. His present is our past, and also our present.

Chronologically, and logically, Joshua follows Moses. But his image has been badly distorted, his name associated with too many wars. Too thirsty for victory, he seems to have believed, as most commanders before and after him, that the end justifies all means. We find Joshua disturbing. Implicated in too many military conflicts, sending too many men to kill or be killed, he seems to personify the victorious but merciless conqueror whom we, naively, would prefer not to find among the founders of Jewish history.

We read the book bearing his name and find ourselves transported from battlefield to battlefield, from execution to hanging, from punishment to vengeance. Lost among cities in ruins and disfigured corpses, we prefer not to look.

Prophecy and poetry appeal more than warfare. Even the talmudic storytellers paid Joshua a minimum of attention. But once we begin piecing together his portrait, drawing on various biblical and midrashic sources, a different Joshua comes into view.

At first it seems difficult to abide by his laws, which are, admittedly, harsh. Then, as one rereads the story of his life, the legend of his legend, one discovers in him depths not seen before. The glorious conquerer emerges as a man of feeling, a lonely man whose heart is heavy and sad.

The Book of Joshua is the greatest chronicle of war in history. Dramatic, suspenseful, colorful, informative, its place in Scripture is unique. Though more revered than many others, including the Judges and the Prophets, few are as controversial. Who wrote it? Some say that Joshua did—with the exception, of course, of the last passage, the one dealing with his death and burial. Others suggest Samuel, Ezra, or Nehemiah as its authors.

The scope is wide, the intensity real. The pace is quick, harrowing. Factual and direct, the book is a report divided into three parts: the conquest of the land, its partition, and the renewed covenant at

Shechem.

The story is about Joshua, yet the towering figure of Moses is present on every page, in every incident: Moses is the perfect master, Joshua the perfect disciple. They are the principal heroes of the tale, although there are others, less famous and less important but, nonetheless, vital for the progression of the story. Some are righteous, others wicked. Some are allowed to live, some die in battle, others after the battle. There is a major storyline, there are secondary plots; there is even a place for romanticism.

We watch as Joshua is cast in his master's mold and follows in his steps. We are led to believe that the two leaders had everything in common, that even their destinies were similar, quasi-identical. "All that happened to the one," says the Talmud, "happened to the other." They endured similar trials, disenchantments, and agonies; they were jubilant and angry for the same reasons; they created the same symbols and nourished the same dreams, except that Joshua succeeded in reaching the Promised Land. Moses' spirit accompanied him even there. The text puts particular emphasis on the fact that Moses had a share in all the events occurring after his death: "Just as the Lord had commanded His servant Moses, so Moses had charged Joshua; and so Joshua did; he left nothing undone of all that the Lord had commanded Moses."

The expression *Kaasher tziva adoshem beyad Moshe*, "as the Lord had commanded Moses" is repeated frequently. Joshua is Moses' extension, the executor of his will. Both reacted the same way to God and Israel. Moses belonged to the tribe of Levi but felt responsible for the entire people; Joshua belonged to the tribe of Ephraim but took charge of the entire nation.

Both concluded covenants, both left testaments, and both died before finishing their task. Also: both witnessed—and provoked—miracles. Moses may have performed a larger number of miracles, but Joshua's were just as spectacular. Which was more impressive: to make a people walk across the Red Sea, or to order the sun and the moon to stand still, and be obeyed? Both were men of total faith and commitment, yet Joshua, in his own words, starts out as *mesharet Moshe*, "Moses' servant" or "assistant." Only later does he become Joshua, a leader in his own right; first, he too had to prove himself.

For archaeologists, geographers, and military historians alike, the book offers invaluable information. Modern-day Israeli generals admit that, had it not been for their knowledge of Joshua's tactics, some of their military operations in defense of their country might have failed. Diplomats and politicians, too, claim the Book of Joshua as a valuable reference. The Talmud views it as a depository of the Jewish right to the land. "Had the Jews not sinned," says the Talmud, "the five books of Moses and that of Joshua alone would have been preserved." Why the Book of Joshua? Because it constitutes the national and legal archives of the Jewish people. Isaiah, Jeremiah, Psalms, Amos, Zephaniah: were it not for the sins of our forebears, they would have found no publisher.

And yet, the Book of Joshua lacks the vision and fire that change simple words into effective prose, into acts of destiny. It also lacks poetry. To be more precise, its strength lies in its presentation of facts.

Perhaps this is why Joshua fares so poorly with talmudic legendmakers, with poets and novelists. Perhaps this is why there is almost nothing celebrating Joshua in world literature—except for a Negro spiritual. Many Jewish intellectuals find it difficult to feel empathy for anyone whose life was as marked by violence as it was untouched by poetry.

Joshua was fierce, unyielding, ruthless, but only in war. He could also be gentle, affectionate, generous.

We remember him mainly in one role, that of military commander. Yet he was also prophet, judge, ruler. In the secret bible of the *Shomronim*, he is called king. In *Pirke Avot*, the *Sayings of the Fathers*, his functions are described in spiritual terms: Moses received the Law at Sinai, and passed it on to Joshua, who passed it on to the elders around him, who passed it on to us. Joshua: Moses' and God's vital link to eternity.

Joshua enters Scripture unannounced. All of a sudden, Moses appoints him to lead a military commando unit—Israel's first—to repel an enemy attack. From that moment on, the two men are inseparable.

Fewer biographical details are available about Joshua than about most biblical figures. We see him only when he is in the limelight, when called upon to perform specific tasks. Was he married? If yes, which is doubtful, he left no sons to inherit his position. Some commentators, taking advantage of their poetic license, tell us he married Rahab, the woman

Five Biblical Portraits

who made Jericho famous. But why would he have married her? To be more precise: why would some talmudic sages have wanted him to marry her? Perhaps because bachelors do not usually fare well in Jewish history. Anyway, there is no trace of such an event in Scripture, but the story itself shows both Joshua and the talmudists as romantic figures: Joshua conquers Jericho and in turn is conquered by its most engaging woman.

His father was named Nun, whom the text does not bother to identify; whereas in Scripture names always signify something, that name in itself means nothing, nor does it reappear in the Bible. His mother seems to have had no name at all.

The reader is somewhat more fortunate when his research leads him into midrashic fantasy. There he finds, as always, if not an answer, then at least . . . a story. In the beginning, the Hebrews had no problems in Egypt. They lived well and in peace with their neighbors. Then one man of the tribe of Ephraim had a dream in which God told him that the children of Israel were meant to be free and destined to become heroic warriors. He shared the dream with his friends, and they with theirs—until eventually they decided to rise up against Egyptian bondage and choose freedom. That is how it all began: with a dream dreamt by Joshua's father. In other words: Joshua was fortunate in having had both a brilliant teacher and an imaginative father.

However, Scripture mentions only the teacher and his influence on Joshua, which is all-encompassing. In fact, Joshua comes to life only when Moses

10

rests his eyes on him.

We read: "Amalek attacked Israel, and Moses told Joshua, 'Choose us some men to rout the aggressor.' "

From this sentence we learn several things. Joshua's life-story begins with a combat mission. Without asking for explanations, without uttering a word, without questioning the order to fight at the head of inexperienced soldiers, Joshua obeyed. He engaged Amalek in combat and defeated him. For the first time in its short history, Israel fought and, for the first time, won. So important was this first military triumph that Moses was ordered to write it down in his book.

The Jews fought and won; this sounds improbable. The aggressors had weapons, but did Joshua and his men have any? If so, from what stores and arsenals? From the Egyptian army! At the Red Sea, the Jews had seized a considerable booty of jewels and precious stones and also of weapons, which were used by Joshua in his counterattack against Amalek.

We do not know why Joshua was chosen for this first combat mission. Moses must have had his reasons. Yet he took a chance. What if Joshua were a poor officer? How could Moses risk losing his first battle with Israel's archenemy? Did he make use of his prophetic powers? No, only of his common sense. Let us reread the text: "And Moses told Joshua, 'Go and choose us some men to rout the aggressor.' " Joshua's first mission was not to go into battle but to choose men for battle. That was the test Moses had prepared for him: whom would he select? A

11

leader's first and foremost talent must be to recognize quality in people and know intuitively how, where, and when to use them.

Moses was right. Joshua was able, loyal, discreet, trustworthy: he possessed all the qualities of a perfect aide-de-camp or chief-of-staff. The two men stayed together and were close as only master and disciple can be. To Joshua, Moses was most of all a teacher. And to Moses, Joshua was a younger brother, an ally, a friend on whom he could always rely.

Joshua was very young when Moses noticed him. The term *Naar* suggests an adolescent. He never left the tent where Moses had his official and private quarters. When Moses received visitors or delegates, Joshua was there, as he was when Moses was alone—face to face with God. Joshua's great personal virtue was that he never disturbed Moses, never weighed on him; his presence never interfered with Moses' understandable need for solitude.

In his circle, Joshua was a leader in his own right. When Moses sent the official leaders of the twelve tribes to scout the land of Canaan, Joshua was among them. That intelligence mission—the first in history—ended poorly. Remember? The majority report was factual and depressing: it stated, the land is beautiful; it is rich; it is the land of milk and honey—and wine, but it is not ours; it belongs to people who are already there; and they are strong; they are giants; in their eyes we seemed like grasshoppers.

Commented the celebrated Rebbe Mendel of Kotzk: "Why was God angry with the scouts? They told the truth after all, or, at least, they told the truth as they saw it. Why were they punished?" And he answered: "God was angry not because of the factual report but because of its interpretation. Why did they care about what other people were thinking of them? They looked like grasshoppers in their eyes —so what? He was angry because they attached an exaggerated importance to the impression they made— and that was their mistake, and their sin."

Joshua and his friend Caleb, son of Jephunneh, represented the minority: two against ten. Of the twelve, they alone had faith in the future. They sided with Moses, with God. Their reward: of all those who left Egypt, they alone entered the Promised Land.

There Caleb withdraws into the background, and Joshua dominates the stage. Messenger and spokesman, interpreter of God's will, military commander, master tactician and strategist: nothing is done without his approval, nothing is undertaken without his blessing.

He resembles his master in all things, except that luck is forever on his side. Unopposed, above criticism, beyond suspicion, he succeeds where Moses has failed. His scouts do not bring back depressing intelligence reports; he does leave the desert; he has no problems with his people—they do not complain, they do not seek golden calves, they do not regret having left exile, they willingly accept the hardships of war, and its discipline. With rare exceptions, the people show themselves worthy of their mission: they all seem aware of living privileged events and epoch-making experiences.

While Moses had to go through innumerable crises and torments, some caused by God and others by Israel, and more often by both, for Joshua everything was simple. In war everything is simple: what is war if not a vast process of simplification?

When Israel obeys the Law, Israel wins. When Jews transgress, they lose. Thus Joshua found it both necessary and convenient to read the Torah to his people before leading them into battle. As a result, his men fought better because they knew what they were fighting for, and for whom.

But to have God on one's side in the battlefield may not always be enough; one also needs military skill—or genius—to make use of the chances offered by God. And Joshua is a military genius. His wars are all textbook wars. Militarily, Joshua remains unsurpassable.

Let us examine his first campaign, his first independent operation, against the well-defended fortress of Jericho. Because of topography, its capture is vital. The temptation must have been there for Joshua to pray for miracles; he uses tactics instead. First, he establishes a tight siege around the city: "None went out and none came in." Then, he manages to introduce spies into the place, and their mission is to report on the defenses and the defenders, their weaponry and their morale. Here too, his spies are luckier than Moses' for they stumble upon a beautiful woman, without whom no spy-thriller can ever be complete. Her name is Rahab; she is hospitable by nature and also by profession. She saves them from Jericho's counterespionage agents, hides them while the search goes on, then helps them return to Joshua's headquarters. As a reward, she is promised her life.

Second phase: Joshua speaks to the troops and to the nation as a whole. To strengthen the national will, he reminds them of their moral heritage and of the miracles yet to come; a master of symbols, he asks for spectacular gestures: twelve stones—symbolizing the twelve tribes—are carried across the river; the males are circumcised, or circumcised again; as it happens to be the month of Nissan, Passover is being celebrated, collectively, under the bluest of blue skies. Joshua's goal is clear: he wants to implant into his people the absolute conviction that their cause is just and their mission and its fulfillment holy. From the moment they cross the Jordan, they are entering sacred time and sacred ground.

Third and last phase: the attack on the besieged city is prepared, using clever and effective methods of psychological warfare. The story, as told in the Book of Joshua, is imbued with realism. One sees the front, watches the defenders, senses the expectation of the assaulting troops, hears the orders; one has the feeling of being there, on the spot, as eyewitness or participant.

"... And God said to Joshua, 'Let all your troops march around the city and complete one circuit of the city. Do this six days, with seven priests carrying seven ram's horns preceding the Ark. On the seventh day, march around the city seven times, with the priests blowing the horns. And when a long blast is sounded on the horn—as soon as you hear that sound of the horn—all the people shall give a mighty shout. Thereupon the city wall will collapse, and the people shall advance, every man straight ahead.'

"Joshua, son of Nun, summoned the priests and said to them, 'Take up the Ark of the Covenant, and let seven priests carrying seven ram's horns precede the Ark of the Lord.' And he instructed the people, 'Go forward, march around the city, with the vanguard marching in front of the Ark of the Lord.' When Joshua had instructed the people, the seven priests . . . advanced before the Lord, blowing their horns; and the Ark of the Lord's Covenant followed them. The vanguard marched in front of the priests who were blowing the horns, and the rear guard marched behind the Ark, with the horns sounding all the time. But Joshua's orders to the rest of the people were, 'Do not shout, do not let your voices be heard, and do not let a sound issue from your lips until the moment that I command you, "Shout!" Then you shall shout.'

"So he had the Ark of the Lord go around the city and complete one circuit; then they returned to camp and spent the night in camp. Joshua rose early the next day; and the priests took up the Ark of the Lord, while the seven priests . . . marched in front of the Ark of the Lord, blowing the horns as they marched. The vanguard marched in front of them, and the rear guard marched behind the Ark of the Lord, with the horns sounding all the time. And so they marched around the city on the second day and returned to the camp. They did this for six days.

"On the seventh day, they rose at daybreak and

marched around the city seven times; that was the only day they marched around the city seven times. On the seventh round, as the priests blew the horns, Joshua commanded the people, 'Shout, for the Lord has given you the city. . . .' When the people heard the sound of the horns, the people raised a mighty shout and the walls collapsed. The people rushed into the city, every man straight in front of him, and they captured the city."

Tactically, psychologically, Joshua's operation is a masterstroke. Imagine the besieged inhabitants, their surprise, their puzzlement, then their worry, their anguish. They do not understand what is happening outside the walls. What are the invaders doing? Why are they circling and circling around the walls— and why silently? Why aren't they attacking? And why is the silence getting thicker and thicker? What is the meaning, what is the power of so much silence? And why are they breaking it all of a sudden? What did make the walls come tumbling down: the shouting, or the silence that preceded it? The element of surprise was so strong that the fortress hardly opposed the attack. It was captured without effort.

At this point, Joshua's greatness is still measured in military terms. So too his shortcomings, for he will lose the next battle. His mistake, like that of many generals throughout the centuries, was to fight old battles in new wars.

The attack on a place named Ai was a blunder. Joshua's triumphant troops were overconfident.

Again, spies were sent ahead. But their report was complacent, overoptimistic: one can almost imagine their smiles as they tell their commander not to worry; after all, they defeated mighty Jericho. This tiny position stands no chance, they say, we don't even need our entire force. Two, three thousand soldiers will do. A poor assessment: the offensive is a disaster. Joshua's task force is repelled and thirty-six casualties are left behind.

Joshua takes it badly: What went wrong? Who was to blame? Why did God turn His face away? What is the use of fighting without God—or against God? Joshua is desperate, but God reassures him: the setback is only temporary—an accident, so to speak. Israel has sinned, that is all. Things went wrong because Israel went astray. "Who sinned?" asks Joshua. "Do not ask Me," says God, according to the Talmud. "Whom do you take Me for, an informer?" Still, God does help Joshua pinpoint the culprit. The entire nation presented itself to Joshua and marched before him, tribe after tribe, household after household. Finally, Joshua located the sinner in the tribe of Judah—in the family, then in the person of Achan, who, in the end, had to confess: "I saw among the spoils a fine Shinar mantle, two hundred pieces of silver, and a wedge of gold weighing fifty shekels, and I coveted them and took them. They are buried in the ground in my tent, with the silver under it." Then, "Joshua, all Israel with him, took Achan son of Zerah, and the silver, the mantle, and the gold, his sons and daughters, and his ox, his ass, and his flock, and his tent, all his belongings and brought them up

to the valley of Achor. And Joshua said: 'What calamity you have brought upon us, the Lord will bring
upon you this day.' And all Israel pelted him with
stones—they put them to the fire and stoned them."

Now Joshua planned a new offensive—which was
as brilliant as the previous one was not. Thirty thousand men, all valiant warriors, lay in ambush behind
the city, while Joshua and his task force approached
the city in a mock frontal attack. As they did the first
time, the soldiers of Ai came out to repel Joshua, and
his men fled, just as they had done the first time.
Falling into the trap, the soldiers of Ai now repeated
Joshua's previous mistake: they did exactly what they
had done during the first battle; they pursued the
assailants, who drew them further and further away
from the city. When Joshua's main force of 30,000
warriors dashed out of their ambush and seized
the empty city, it was too late for its defenders to
turn around: they were caught between two armies,
and quickly destroyed.

The battle of Jericho announced Joshua's military genius, that of Ai confirmed it. His star rose
higher and higher. Good planning, daring maneuvers
and a spirit of comradeship, solidarity, and self-sacri-
fice led to more and more victories.

Joshua was the perfect commander. He never left
his troops; he always set the example. He was probably the first Jewish officer to lead his men into war
shouting: "*Acharai*—follow me!" Before the second
attack against the fortress of Ai, he spent the night
working out the last details. From the text itself we
almost see him going around the camp, inspecting

the companies, talking with the officers. Instead of waiting with the passive and secure ambushing force, he chose to lead the more dangerous frontal attack. Furthermore, he took the trouble to explain every stage, every move of every operation to his entire army—beforehand. He involved them in the decision-making process; he gave them a sense of pride and responsibility. Wasn't he afraid that someone might betray him, sell his military secrets to the enemy? How could he trust every single man and woman? How could he be sure of an entire people? He was sure—and therein, too, lay his greatness. Whatever he did, he did with the soldiers and with their officers and their families; Israel was never so united as under Joshua's rule. The people responded to him: they followed him not blindly but with their eyes wide open. And together they marched forward. Quick, audacious, unpredictable, Joshua and his men appeared wherever the enemy expected them the least, struck, and went on. Irresistible and implacable, implacable and pitiless.

Thirty-one kings and their armies occupied the land of Canaan; Joshua vanquished them all. Not one survived. Some were slain in battles, some were hanged. Occasionally, his brutality seems gratuitous. Five kings hid in a cave while the combat was still raging. Joshua shut the entrance to the cave and returned to the battlefield. When it was all over, he presented the five royal prisoners-of-war to the people, and his officers were told to "come forward and place your feet on the necks of these kings."

After that, the five defeated rulers were impaled on five stakes and put to death.

Why so much brutality? Why such lack of magnanimity toward the beaten enemy? Why did all the battles fought and won by Joshua end in mass executions and massacres? One reads Joshua's heroic exploits and admires them, but with embarrassment. Again and again one asks: Why, why? Why did he exterminate all the inhabitants of Jericho? Why did he slay all the citizens of Ai?

Of course, one may argue that Joshua was no less rigorous with his own people. One may recall Achan to the witness stand: he was Jewish, belonging to a prestigious family of a prestigious tribe, and yet, when he sinned, he was punished—punished for having transgressed God's order not to profit from other people's tragedy, for not having confessed right away, for thus having caused the entire nation to be suspect, for having given the impression that Israel was fighting for gold and silver and not for history.

But the argument can be turned around: the punishment was too harsh. If Achan was indicted and condemned, he deserved it. But why was his family pelted with stones? Why were his children punished? And why did no one question the justice of the verdict? What happened to the eternal protesters on whom we could—and still can—count to speak up in the name of truth and justice, in the name of conscience?

True, Joshua acted on God's orders. But then,

why was God so cruel? Why were His orders so merciless?

Of course, one may say: Why blame Joshua? Blame war. He never waged war for the sake of war. He hated war and tried to avoid it.

Yes, he tried. Before setting out on his conquest of Canaan, Joshua dispatched to its kings three letters with three options: evacuate the land; stay and accept Jewish rule; or—and this was the third and last option—stay and fight.

Some chose exile. The Byzantine historian of the sixth century, Procopius, mentions some Phoenicians who, fearing Joshua, left Canaan and went to Egypt. From there they moved to Libya, where they settled permanently near a place named Tigisis, where two marble pillars were allegedly found with the following inscription: "We are those who fled before Joshua ben Nun's bandits." The Talmud mentions another tribe, that of Loz, who had the good sense to heed Joshua's injunction and leave voluntarily for other distant shores. As a reward, says the Talmud, all members of that tribe escaped the Angel of Death forever.

There were also the Gibeonites, who chose to stay and submit to Jewish rule, and live in peace.

But most decided to stay and fight. Joshua's troops were small in number: showing mercy would have been mistaken for weakness. They had to be ruthless. Kill or be killed: that was the international law, the law of destiny. For Canaan to be conquered, its inhabitants had to disappear. That is how God willed it. Had the natives fled or collaborated, they would have remained alive. In other words, they had but themselves to blame. They had been foolish to resist.

Naturally, the question may be asked differently: what right did Joshua have to impose such choices on them in the first place? Didn't the land belong to them? No, affirms the Talmud, the land of Canaan had belonged to Israel since creation; the Canaanites were only temporary caretakers. Thus Joshua's wars were not wars of aggression or conquest but of reconquest. Their aim: to reclaim possession of what rightfully belonged to them. All Jews shared that conviction then; they were going home, they were not invaders. That is why Joshua repeatedly reminded them of God's covenant and His promise: their fight was part of a divine design. In God's scheme, the people and the land of Israel have always been one. Had Joshua felt a foreigner in Canaan, he and his men would not have fought as bravely.

But what about the actual inhabitants of Canaan? Weren't they victims nevertheless? Yes, God's victims. It was God who gave their land away to Abraham and his children; that is when the first injustice was committed. What happened later was nothing but commentary.

Remove history from Joshua and his wars seem inadmissible, even incomprehensible. Seen in the light of history, he could do nothing else, and nothing different.

Israel was occupied by Canaanites, so it was Joshua's sacred duty to liberate it: the war of conquest was, to his mind, a war of liberation.

23

As for the Canaanites, perhaps they had their own chroniclers who described the events from their viewpoint. The Jewish version is what we know, from the Book of Joshua, which lacks both objectivity and poetry. The book is inspired but not inspiring—why? It lacks the extra prophetic dimension which we find in all other books of our sacred tradition—why?

Here we must raise the question of war and Jewish attitudes towards it. Jews are against war and always have been. The reason is obvious. From the time of Joshua, whenever two nations went to battle, no matter who won, the Jews always lost. Religious or territorial wars, ideological or racial wars, Jews were forever caught in the crossfire, forever among the defeated, the victims. No wonder they aspired to peace above all else.

The literature of war in Jewish tradition is astonishingly poor: ancient Jewish military handbooks have disappeared. On the other hand, no theme is richer and more persistent than that of peace. Whereas the seal of God is truth, His name is peace. God created the universe, according to the Midrash, for for the sole purpose of bringing peace to mankind. All that is contained in the Torah must contribute to peace; even the passages evoking Jewish wars were written only to preserve peace. All virtues granted to man by God have limitations, says the Midrash, with the exception of two: Torah and peace, which must be—and are—boundless.

The Talmud authorizes lies only when they are

told in the interest of peace. The *Sifrei* goes further, stating that for the sake of peace, one may worship idols and even pay tribute to heathens.

No tradition, no history, is as peace-oriented as Judaism. Cain and Abel? Two brothers waging war: whoever kills, kills his brother. As a result, the tradition never considered any war holy. Even when war is an absolute necessity, it is still perceived as an aberration, a denial of God's name.

Naturally, Jews have had their share of heroes: Samson, Saul, David, the Maccabees, and Bar-Kochba, but all of them represented more than military bravery; they represented another measure of spirituality. Even so, they are to be admired but not necessarily imitated. Sages, not warriors, have been Jewish models of behavior.

War is evil by definition. It moves man to revert to primary darkness. War has always been a convenient pretext to abolish all laws, all prohibitions, and give man license to lie, shame, mutilate, humiliate, and kill—with good conscience. In the name of war, man feels free, and proud, to violate social contracts and divine commandments. War turns into a primitive show: on the one side the good, who must live; on the other the wicked, who must vanish.

And yet, at times, war may seem inevitable and justified—defensive war, that is, which had to be decided by the king, and ratified by the full Sanhedrin. Then, and only then, did Jewish leaders have the authority to proclaim total mobilization and a state of emergency. Then, and only then, did Jews pull together all their energies: even spiriting bridegrooms away from wedding ceremonies. When the nation is in danger, all must do the impossible to save it. When survival was at stake, Jews fought, and fought well. From Joshua down to our contemporary heroes, Jews have had to learn how to defend themselves.

Was that not the situation in Joshua's time? Did he have a choice? At that point in history, everything was still possible. Joshua could have turned to God and said: "Master of the Universe, listen to me, if bloodshed and violence are the price for national sovereignty, thank You—get Yourself another nation, not the descendants of Abraham and Isaac and Jacob, not the disciples of Moses, who taught them to live and let live." Then Jewish survival would have become God's problem, not Joshua's.

But Joshua did not object to war and that is our problem with him. How could he shed so much blood and spread so much violence? Why didn't he—the man who caused the sun to stand still in Gibeon and the moon to wait in the Valley of Ajalon—ask God to give Israel its Promised Land through a few old-fashioned inexpensive miracles? And spare Israel —let alone the Canaanites—the traumatizing effects of military conquest? Couldn't God have done in Canaan what He did at the Red Sea, namely, fight for His people—instead of making His people fight?

The answer is simple: He could have but chose not to. He did not want to make it too easy for Israel. He wanted Israel to want the land of Israel, fight for it, pay for it with blood—Jewish and non-Jewish. For Israel to become a nation, it had to do what other nations have had to do since time immemorial. Perhaps God wanted Israel to wage this war once and for all, so as to lose all taste for war.

To be more specific: nations, like human beings, occasionally purged themselves of their inherent violent, destructive and/or self-destructive impulses. Some did so in the beginning, others somewhat later. Jews belong to the first category. They began their adventure in mankind's history as a conquering nation that found it necessary to build its dreams on other people's ruins; they changed later and turned Judaism into a powerful quest for humanism. Other civilizations did the reverse. They began by preaching peace, brotherhood, and love, and with the passage of time indulged in large-scale destruction—in the very name of peace, brotherhood, and love.

Yes, Jews waged war once upon a time; the Book of Joshua is here to prove it. It is full of bloodshed and violence, and it does lack poetry. But its very lack of literary beauty can be seen as a virtue. Joshua won many battles but the Bible does not boast about them. That is true of all Jewish wars. The prophets refused to sanctify them, the poets declined to romanticize them. Songs were written to celebrate miracles, not wars. In his farewell address to the nation, as he was looking back at his life, Joshua—significantly —omitted any mention of his conquests: he wanted to be remembered as prophet, not as conquerer.

Viewed from this perspective, one comes to realize that Joshua was secretive, imaginative, poetically unhappy, yearning for friendship and human warmth and serenity. The dreamer has seen his dream fulfilled, or at least partly fulfilled—and now what?

Joshua was "old and stricken in years." The country "rested from war," yet "very much land remained to be claimed and possessed."

So Joshua invited "all Israel, their elders and their heads, and their judges, and their officers" to come—for the last time—and listen to his farewell; he knew and they knew that this would be their last meeting.

What does he tell them? To take care of the land? To stick together? To be good Jews? To cling to God? To remember him? To preserve the heritage? To maintain the memory of their nation? To protect the Torah? No! He tells them ... to start all over again. To make up their minds. To speak up and commit themselves either to God or to other gods! "If you dislike the God of our fathers," he tells them, "serve someone else!"

This is unique! A choice—now? After the exodus from Egypt, after the revelation at Sinai, after the miracles in the desert, after the battles, after so many tragedies and triumphs, Joshua offers them the possibility of closing the book and ... beginning again.

That is an act of unbelievable audacity! How could he bring himself to gamble and risk everything? He did, and in so doing he taught us yet another essential aspect of the Jewish tradition: to be Jewish is not a one-time choice; we choose for ourselves every day. How did Israel Zangwill put it? We are not the chosen people, but the choosing people.

That special moment—that last battle, the inner battle—brings us close to Joshua. But that is not all.

One becomes aware of his humanity when one studies his relationship with individual human beings. First, with Moses, whom he admired and loved. And yet, he had to hurt his master by succeeding him in his lifetime. When Moses refused to die, says the Talmud, God made him jealous of Joshua. Joshua, God's unhappy instrument; Joshua, the leader against his will. God's explanation to Moses that he must die, to allow Joshua to take over, meant to Joshua that so long as he himself would not take over, Moses would go on living. For him to rule, his beloved teacher had to die. Imagine his guilt feelings, his sadness.

His relationship with his friend Caleb attracts us. Together, the two of them contested the reports of Moses' official scouts and helped him convince the people that the land was indeed good and hospitable. Yet forty-five years later, Caleb came to Joshua asking for a piece of property, saying, "Remember what I did and said in those critical hours." *I*, not *we*. Joshua could have corrected him but did not, and granted his request.

His generosity toward Rahab-the-harlot was equally admirable: in the middle of war he remembered his promise and kept it. She and her family were spared.

When Joshua was first appointed by Moses, he was sneered at by the elderly dignitaries. "Look at Moses and look at his successor," they said. "They are like the sun and the moon—what a shame, what a shame." It was not easy to succeed Moses. Joshua did so against his will—just as he waged war, later, against his will, only because God ordered him to do so. He was a tragic figure, whose triumphs brought him no happiness; on the contrary, they made him sadder, lonelier. He did not even complete his task; some parts of the land were still occupied. Joshua felt weary. He had seen too much suffering on too many battlefields; he had learned the terrible price of victory.

He died alone, utterly alone. He was buried in a place called *Har gaash*—a kind of volcano. The Talmud sees this as valid proof that something essential to our understanding of the man has been omitted from the biblical narrative; it comments on Israel's shocking ingratitude toward its old leader. In the name of Rav Jehuda, the Talmud says, "And Joshua was buried at the north of *Har-gaash*, the angry mountain. Why was the mountain angry? Because God, in His outrage, was about to punish His people by burying them under the mountain. And why was He outraged? Because no one bothered to come to Joshua's funeral. Why not? Because they were too busy. One was busy in his garden, the other in his vineyard, the third with his coal." Strange but true: Joshua was Israel's leader in war; when the war ended, they needed him no more.

Poor Joshua. His last battle was against "the giants" of the mountain. Were they real or part of his nightmare? Did he have any regrets? How did he foresee the future? Could he have known that his war—

which he had hoped to be Israel's first and last—would not be the last?

When all is said and done, Joshua's wars are presented as wars, not as religion. His book about war is a book against war, a tale of bloodshed to teach resistance to bloodshed.

When King Nebuchadnezzar of Babylon, who destroyed the Temple, felt the urge to sing, the angel Michael slapped him in his face. Destruction and singing do not go together.

When the Jews crossed the Red Sea, the angels felt like singing, and God told them to keep quiet: "My creatures are drowning and all you can think about is singing!"

But then, if God cared that much about the Egyptians, why did He drown them? That is for Him to answer. But the angels were wrong to use the death of human beings—however wicked—for purposes of lyrical theology. Death must never be glorified.

Poor Joshua, glorious Joshua. He was forced to win so many battles—with no one around to say thank you. Except God.

Elijah

And it came to pass that when the Almighty God of Israel chose to recall His prophet in a tempest of fire, Elijah left Gilgal accompanied by his faithful disciple Elisha.

This was to be their last journey together, and both were too aware, too discerning not to know it. They talked little, each lost in his own thoughts. Master and disciple had been close; their imminent separation could only sharpen their sense of loss and suffering. What would become of them, one and the other—one without the other?

Suddenly Elijah turned towards his young companion and said: "Listen, you stay here. I must proceed to Beth-El for God wants me to go there—but you stay here."

Elisha refused, saying: "I swear by God and on your life that I shall not leave you."

Faced with such determination, Elijah did not insist. And both resumed their march towards Beth-El. In silence.

In Beth-El, they were welcomed by young local

prophets who took Elisha aside and asked him: "Do you know that today is the Day—the Day singled out by the Almighty? Your Master will be taken away from you. Are you aware of this?" — "Yes, I am," Elisha replied. He said no more, nor did the young prophets.

Then Elijah turned once more toward his companion: "Stay here, Elisha," he said. "I must go on to Jericho—I must, not you. Stay here, please."

"No," said Elisha. "I swear by God as I swear on your life that I shall not desert you."

Once more, Elijah did not argue. Was he unhappy with his disciple's stubbornness, his loyalty? He showed no sign of pleasure or displeasure. Together, silently, they resumed their march to Jericho.

There again they were greeted by young prophets. They too drew Elisha aside and questioned him: "Do you know that today is the Day?" — "Yes, I do," replied Elisha. He said no more, nor did the young prophets.

And for the third time Elijah tried to discourage his young friend from following him. "Stay here, please. I must go to the Jordan River for that is where God has sent me. Not you, you stay here."

For the third time Elisha refused: "I swear by God and on your life that I shall not leave you alone —neither here nor anywhere, now or ever."

Thus together they left Jericho and journeyed to the Jordan River, followed at a distance by fifty young prophets, who were determined to witness the event and share it with their friends elsewhere.

Master and disciple walked and walked, halting

only when they reached the river. Elijah removed his mantle and used it to divide the waters, which opened a path for them. "What would you wish me to obtain for you?" Elijah asked his disciple as they crossed the river.— "I would like my powers to be twice as great as yours," said the young disciple.— "That is too much," said Elijah. "But listen and listen well: if you will actually see me go, then you will know that your wish was granted—but only then."

And suddenly it happened. While they were walking, while they were talking, a chariot of fire pulled by horses of fire descended from heaven, and Elijah was seized and swept away. It did not last more than an instant; Elisha found himself alone. Elijah had left him; he had gone to heaven in a whirlwind of flames. And Elisha had seen it all, had understood it all. A cry, profound and painful, left his lips, a cry that was to shake the universe to its foundations: "Father, father, chariots of Israel, and the horsemen thereof!" But no answer was to be heard. No echo. Nothing. Elisha cried but his master was gone. Forever.

Forever? Elisha may have thought so. The fifty prophets, at a distance, may have thought so. But they were all wrong. For, in this case, the unthinkable occurred: Elijah did return among his fellowmen throughout the centuries, so as to remind them of their rights to hope and memory—and to offer men not fascination with death but a taste of immortality.

From the viewpoint of literature, this passage contains the elements of a true masterpiece: rhythm, action, melody, suspense, repetition. We succumb to its intensity. The characters are real; they explode with truth. We see them as they walk together, together for a while, and then separated—and yet inseparable.

The wisdom of the master, the loyalty of his pupil. The prophet's desire to remain alone—literally and physically alone—in order to confront what he knew would be his unique and supreme encounter with death. Not to be seen then by anyone: that was his wish. To be alone as death is alone, as God is alone. Elijah also wanted to spare his young friend the sight of a diminished old master dying, a victim of God, helpless and lifeless as are all victims of all absolute forces. Elijah loved his young protégé; he wanted to protect him to the last, to shield him from further suffering, from having to carry too many painful memories. "Stay Elisha," he urged him once, twice, three times: "*I* must go—not you." The repetition is heartbreaking. The same scene unfolds three times, the same argument is used three times, only the names are different: Beth-El, Jericho, the river Jordan. And Elisha, entranced by the poetry of the exchange, answers in the same vein; he too repeats his words over and over to emphasize his obstinacy: "I swear by God as I swear on you—I am staying with you." We feel the tension growing and soon it becomes unbearable as we come closer to the dénouement. Elijah is about to leave this world; he knows it, so do we. And Elisha? He knows it too—he knows it even before the young prophets who want to inform him but not his master. The rumor of Elijah's impending departure seems to precede him wherever he goes: today is the Day singled out by God—the day we are all fearing; Elijah is going away, he is leaving us. At first, people merely watch the two men and let them proceed by themselves; then, at Jericho, for the last stage, fifty prophets follow them at a distance, to observe, to see, to report back home.

Then comes the moment of separation. Elijah remains master of his senses and of his role: he wishes to offer his disciple a parting gift, and allows him to name it. And there Elisha surprises us with his answer. He does not say: "What I really, truly wish is that you stay with me—I wish not to be left alone." Nor does he say: "Take me along, let us overcome this decree of separation." Or: "If you must leave me, promise to come back and be with me in this hostile, materialistic, and cynical world." Instead of pleading for his master's life and work, he implores him on his own behalf and for his own personal career: he wants powers. Moreover, he wishes them to be twice as great as those of his master. Is that Elisha's last wish—thus his only wish—his most secret desire? Is this how a loyal and loving disciple says farewell to his teacher: by yearning to surpass him and by telling him this directly? We do not understand Elisha.

Nor do we understand Elijah. Until now, in Scripture, he has appeared as the prophet of anger. Fierce, uncompromising, extremely sensitive, he responds with rage to the slightest provocation. And here, he does not get angry; he is not even offended. What has happened to change him so? Instead of teaching his young pupil manners, or patience, he grants him his wish, or, at least, assures him that his wish might be granted if he sees him go away. This only increases our bewilderment. What is the connection? What is the meaning? Why must Elisha keep his eyes open to become a prophet in his own right? For the first—and last—time in his life, Elijah is speaking in riddles—he who has always spoken his mind frankly and clearly! He whose mission has been to dispel ambiguity! He whose task one day will be to solve all mysteries adds one of his own! Has he really vanished? Has he really ascended into heaven? And what if he simply chose to withdraw from society and resign his official duties?

Elijah: he is present to children and old men alike. In moments of solitude, he emerges to lend wings to our imagination. In moments of joy, he is there to share in it. Elijah: the impossible but necessary hope, the reality of fantasy. Elijah: a poet's dream, a philosopher's challenge. Elijah and his miracles. Elijah and his battles. Elijah and his victories, which are our victories. Elijah, our intercessor. He took God to task and God thanked him for his courage—God, but not the people. The people he defended actually made fun of him.

A few words about the concept, the role, the fabric of the prophet in general. Who is a prophet? Someone who is searching—someone who is being sought. Someone who listens—and who is listened to. Someone who sees people as they are, and as they ought to be. Someone who reflects his time, yet lives outside time.

A prophet is forever awake, forever alert; he is never indifferent, least of all to injustice, be it human or divine, whenever or wherever it may be found. God's messenger to man, he somehow becomes man's messenger to God.

Restless, disquieting, he is forever waiting for a signal, a summons. Asleep, he hears voices and follows visions; his dreams do not belong to him.

Often persecuted, always in anguish, he is alone —even when addressing crowds, when conversing with God or himself, when describing the future or evoking the past.

There is sometimes a theatrical aspect to him; he seems to recite lines written by someone else. And yet, in order for him to be a prophet, he must descend into the very depths of his being. In order for him to be inhabited or penetrated—or invaded—by God, he must be truly, authentically himself.

Hence, a prophet's tragic dimension: having attained the highest degree of self-realization, he gives himself to God. The more he exists, the more he belongs to God, who speaks through his voice and uses him as a link, a bridge, an instrument. The prophet is at once an irritant and a simplifier. What others will think or learn, the prophet already knows; he is the first to know. He is God's sounding board. But, at times, he is the last to know: Elijah spoke and occasionally did not know what he had said, according to the Talmud.

In this respect, Elijah is no exception. He preached, he performed miracles, won many battles and surely many arguments, and yet, unlike most prophets, he lived and lived and lived . . .

But when one scrutinizes the text, one is confronted by elements that are disturbing. The man was never happy, not even in his triumph. Furthermore, he seems to have had no past, no roots. His life was a dramatic passage from eternity to eternity; he came from legend and returned to legend.

Historically, Elijah is a contemporary of Homer. He appears in the biblical narrative thundering, overturning all obstacles, electrifying everything around him. Nobody expected him, but once he was there, he alone mattered.

Who is he, really?

We study the sources—both biblical and talmudic—and certain details, certain traits emerge as significant and revealing. We know, from a passing remark, that he wears a "garment of haircloth, with a girdle of leather about his loins." His hair is long. He has no particular profession; in fact, he is unemployed, homeless, and a bachelor. Physically strong, "he could run ahead of horses for eighteen miles," although his diet is rather poor: we know what he ate and drank in the desert. We also know that he has the perplexing habit of appearing and disappearing under the most unusual circumstances. Daring, imaginative, provocative, he is a masterful stage director: he knows how to impress people and move them to ecstasy.

Such is the biblical portrait of Elijah: tough,

fierce, and cruel, irascible, inflexible, monolithic, a destroyer of false idols and their worshipers. His power of concentration is remarkable. He does not talk; he commands. But when he listens to one person, he listens to no one else. When he is alone, he is the loneliest creature on earth; when surrounded by crowds, he is even lonelier. A man of extremes, he rejects weaknesses and compromises. His severity and rigor are legendary; he hardly ever smiles. More than a person, he is destiny.

The way he expresses himself is always striking. No sermons, no speeches, no discourses on morality. Short, biting sentences: verbal whiplashes. To King Ahab, who confiscates Naboth's garden, he snaps: *Haratzachta vegam yarashta?* "You have killed a man and now you shall get his heritage too?" If that brief opinion is not effective enough, he continues: "Just as the dogs licked the blood of your victim, they will lick yours." To Ahab's successor, Ahaziah, he says: "You will not leave your bed alive." To the officer who has come to arrest him, he says: "A fire from heaven will devour you." And somehow his prophecies always come true.

Elijah inspires fear and awe. Whatever he wants, he gets. Whatever he predicts, happens. Let him open his mouth and the earth will tremble. Let him lift his arm and men, seized with terror, will feel the Angel of Death.

Elijah, a man with no history, makes history by galvanizing it. His mission is to punish complacent kings and their flatterers, to bend the vain and encourage the humble, to show the great how small they are, and the mighty how vulnerable they are. Wherever he appears, one breathes the fury and flame of heaven. Relentless in his fight against injustice, he unmasks hypocrisy and falsehood. Whenever he enters the picture, things are bound to explode.

We know little about Elijah the man, about his father, his place of origin, his teachers, his mentors. Like a character in a play, he reveals himself only by what he does and says on stage. All the rest is mystery. His official identity itself is obscure. Elijah-from-Tishbi. It is doubtful that there was ever a place with such a name. One Talmudic source claims that he was of the priestly tribe. No convincing proof is offered, which enables other tribes to claim him. He belongs to all the tribes, to all of us. He responds to man's eternal need for poetry and his eternal quest for justice.

Let us read from Scripture: There were kings in Israel and Judea, and most of them were mediocre and selfish; some were even worse. In a house divided against itself, spirituality was first to go. Leaders emerged and disappeared in endless wars, intrigues, plots and counterplots. Wars and alliances with Phoenicians and Assyrians, usually for the wrong motives, resulted in increased degradation, idolatry, and more idolatry. The God of Israel was a stranger in His own land.

The most wicked of the kings was Ahab, who sinned more than his father Omri—who sinned more than his father Jeroboam ben Nebat. To secure his alliance with the Phoenicians, Ahab married the Phoenician princess Jezebel, daughter of Priest and King Ethbaal of Sidon. Under her influence, he built pagan temples, opened his palace to false prophets and allowed the reconstruction of Jericho despite Joshua's memorable order.

Ahab goes from sin to sin, from disgrace to disgrace, taking the entire nation—and its history—with him. They were falling lower and lower; nothing and no one could stop them, let alone save them.

And then, all of a sudden, the text says: *Vayomer Eliyahu ha-tishbi mitoshavei gilead el Ahav.* . . . "And Elijah, the Tishbi, citizen of Gilead, addressed King Ahab and told him: 'I swear by the God of Israel that there will be no rain until I so order.' "

Eliyahu-the-Tishbi, citizen of Gilead. Place of birth, unknown. Age, unknown. The text wants him to remain unknown.

Except for his visible qualities. From the opening sentence we learn that Elijah manifested himself through language, through his courage, and also through his faith in his own strength. He knows his threats are not idle.

Thus we know right away not only that Elijah exists, but that he is a prophet. We are there as he confronts the king in person. He tells the king that he is not the mightiest creature; that there are powers that elude him; that there is a will that his will cannot control. "From now on," says Elijah, "I and I alone shall decide when this land will know happiness or hunger; I and I alone shall be the master of the rain that links the skies above to the earth below."

Surely a man of courage, Elijah. He hardly has finished his sentence, however, than he has vanished.

If Ahab answered him or reacted to his threat, it has not been recorded. All we are told is that Elijah spoke and . . . fled. Before we accuse him of cowardice, however, we ought to know that he fled on orders, God's orders. God simply ordered him to go away and hide near the Jordan River. To see no one—and be seen by no one. "Do not worry," God told him, "you will be fed by ravens. And the river will give you its waters. You will live in hiding—but you will live. And lack nothing."

Not so the others. When Elijah's prophecy came true, the three-year drought brought hunger to the land and the people. The earth was thirsty, and so was the prophet. He left his hiding place and found refuge with a widow whom God had ordered to feed him; she was rewarded: she never ran out of food. But her son fell ill, and Elijah was blamed: "It's your fault," she said. "You came and brought my sins to the foreground and thus harmed my son, who is now dying." In Scripture, this angry outburst is incomprehensible.

In the Midrash, it is not. Listen to its interpretation. "Before you came," said the widow, "God loved me because I was virtuous—I mean, compared to others I was, I really was. But compared to you? . . . So it is because of you that God doesn't love me any more. Why did you come here? Why?" Well, Elijah had no choice; he had to cure her son.

A miracle? Yes. Like Moses, whom he resembles in twenty-eight ways, Elijah performs miracles. But this one is of a particular kind: it takes place in quasi-secrecy. Whereas most miracles are meant to impress as many witnesses as possible, this one was witnessed by only three persons, Elijah included. He did the same again later, centuries later, when he comforted, consoled, and saved despair-stricken victims in exile by appearing to them alone.

In Scripture Elijah performed other more public, more spectacular miracles as well. He challenged King Ahab to a public confrontation, a gigantic verbal duel. His language was clear, provocative: "You worship the idols, I serve God—let us see who is alive and who is not."

The entire population was invited to Mount Carmel, especially the false prophets: 400 Baal-worshipers and 450 of Jezebel's house-prophets, so to speak. Facing this assembly was one man, Elijah, who believed in one God, the God of Israel.

And Elijah spoke, and what he said made sense: "You cannot serve both God and Baal; you cannot be both Jewish and anti-Jewish; you cannot believe in your own destiny and in someone else's. You must commit yourself, take a stand. *Ad matai tifsekhu al shtei haseipim!* How long are you going to live in two camps at once?" One must choose. If God is God, follow Him; if Baal is God, follow him.

The people, says the text, did not reply: already then, people preferred to wait, and join the winner.

Elijah himself directed the staging, and his directions are so explicit and so detailed that they offer a rare glimpse into ancient pagan Baal rituals.

Two oxen were brought, and Elijah asked his opponents to choose one and offer it in sacrifice, according to their tradition. Then he would do the same, except that both rites included an offering by fire, which comes from God alone. "Well," said Elijah, "let us see your god and mine at work." The other side accepted the challenge, and lived to regret it. Courteous, Elijah allowed the prophets of Baal to open the contest. They built their altar and prayed for fire. But there was no fire. The priests and prophets implored Baal with all their might; there was still no fire. In fact, says the Midrash, there was nothing. Only silence—like the silence that reigned when God gave the Law: the birds did not sing, the oxen did not bellow, the angels did not fly, the sea was calm, no creature made a sound. God caused creation to be silent, and void, and empty, as if no living thing existed. For if anyone had spoken, the priests would have said: "Baal has answered us!"

But Baal remained mute, absent. At this point, Elijah began to mock them: "Perhaps you are not shouting loudly enough! He is asleep—or away! Wake him up . . ."

The prophet's irony may seem unfair and therefore out of character. Is it proper to ridicule a defeated adversary? But as we scrutinize the text more closely, we realize our mistake: the false prophets are not yet defeated—since Elijah has not yet performed his miracle. Since he was not sure that his plea would be heard and that he would obtain fire from heaven, he simply was pushing them to continue their efforts with increased vigor, not to give in too soon. And they did not. They howled and shouted, and lacerated their flesh in collective madness for hours and hours. Finally, at dusk, they admitted defeat.

Then came Elijah's turn. He "rebuilt" the altar with twelve stones to illustrate the unity of Israel's twelve tribes. And he implored God's help: "God of Abraham, Isaac, and Jacob, prove to us here that You are the God of Israel ... *Anéni adoshem, anonéni*— answer me, God." The Midrash interprets this poetically: "Answer me so that people will understand Your part in the miracle. And the entire people saw God's answer; the entire people saw a fire that came down from heaven to accept and consume Elijah's offering." The story does not end here. After Elijah's victory, he ordered the people to massacre all the false prophets.

The Midrash is not too concerned with the tragic fate of the false prophets, surely not as much as with the fate of the poor oxen. Listen to its description of the event: In order to be absolutely fair, Elijah suggested to the prophets of Baal to choose two twin oxen and then to let fate decide which of them would be sacrificed to God and which one to Baal. The first gave no resistance and followed Elijah as would a friend. As for the second one, he simply refused to play his part. Not only didn't he agree to follow the false prophets but he remained riveted to the ground—and no power in the world could move him. All the priests and prophets, and their assistants, tried—and failed.

The scene would have been comical enough without the ox who felt the need to explain his behavior to Elijah: "Look," he said, "here we are, twin brothers, born of the same mother; we grew up together, we were fed together, we walked together in the same fields and rested in the same shade—so tell me: why am I to be discriminated against? Why is my brother being offered to the eternal God and I to a silly idol? Why should my brother sanctify the living God while I anger Him? Is this fair or just, tell me?" Elijah understood: the ox was right—but still, the show had to go on! So he tried to comfort the poor ox: "Do not worry," he told him, "you too will sanctify God's name—you by being offered to Baal and your brother by being offered to God; you both have lived and will die in His service and for His sake." Still the ox was not convinced: "I understand you," he replied, "but I am not going to Baal voluntarily! Since I must go—you make me go! You deliver me into their hands!" And Elijah had no choice but to comply.

Naturally God won and the people exclaimed: *Adoshem hu ha Elokim,* "God is God." And clouds covered the sky and it began to rain. Once more earth gave man his sustenance. All was well—creation had reconciled itself with its Creator.

As for Elijah, things were not any easier for him afterwards. True, he had won, but he was not out of danger. Once again he had to flee. What a strange destiny: when he lost, he fled, and when he won, he also fled. There was a price on his head and he went underground. But who was hunting him down? King Ahab had repented at Mount Carmel. Elijah paid him due homage as king, and, as was the custom, ran in front of his chariot. It was Jezebel who would persecute Elijah, God's true messenger.

She was his real and most vicious enemy—she more than her husband. Now she was determined to avenge the massacre of her loyal priests, an event she had not been aware of until it was too late. Had she been there, Elijah's task surely would have been more difficult.

The confrontation on Mount Carmel had been planned and executed behind Jezebel's back. Elijah wanted her to be absent during the momentous confrontation, not because he was afraid of her, but because her husband was.

In that royal family, clearly it was the woman who reigned. Jezebel ruled over her husband and therefore over the nation. It was she who made the most important—and bloodiest—decisions; it was she who ordered the slaughter of the true prophets of the Jewish people, she who built altars to Baal, she who manipulated people against people, and all against the God of Israel. If that Jewish kingdom became indifferent to its own mission, it was her doing. Ahab was too much in love to protest—and she made him more and more dependent on her. From biblical and talmudic sources we draw an accurate picture of her as sensuous but sexually frustrated. She had a taste for luxury and power, she loved to participate in other people's rituals such as weddings and funerals. Some sources indicate that she often used strange and daring methods to arouse her husband's passion—we are given graphic details. Clearly, Ahab was so addicted to her that he allowed her to run the business of government.

Jezebel charted the nation's domestic policy, its foreign policy, and its theology—with Ahab's permission. He never objected, never confronted her, even on the battlefield. We are told that he was a great commander, but only when she was not around; he was a weakling, but only when she was around.

The best example can be found in the episode of the Garden of Naboth. There once lived a man named Naboth, whose garden was close to the royal garden. King Ahab wanted that garden and offered to pay Naboth, who did not wish to give it up. Ahab then offered him another garden, elsewhere. "Sorry," said Naboth, "I do not feel like moving." He simply wanted to stay in his own garden, in his own home, which reminded him of his childhood, his parents and theirs. Ahab insisted and persisted, but Naboth remained firm.

Ahab felt sad, deprived, frustrated—as only kings can. He returned to his palace unhappy, ill, angry. He went straight to bed without eating his supper. "What is happening to you?" asked his wife. "Why are you in such a bad mood? Who did what to you? Why don't you eat?" He explained, complaining over the stubbornness of Naboth.

"Is that all?" said Jezebel. "But, my dear husband, if that is all that worries you, then do not take it that badly. Leave it to your dear wife, she will take care of it . . ."

And she did take care of Naboth, that is. She arranged a trumped-up trial—the first show trial in Jewish history—using the services of false witnesses, who testified that Naboth had plotted to become a leader. She even managed to convince some people to treat Naboth as a leader so as to build a better case against him in court. The frame-up worked. Naboth became a leader against his will, a defendant against his will. And he was condemned, stoned. And all because Jezebel's husband had wanted a larger garden.

The picture becomes clear: even in this small episode, it was Jezebel who solved Ahab's problem. For all practical purposes she was the leader of the nation; her powers were unchallenged, her decisions irrevocable.

One may assume that Ahab, in moments of lucidity and self-examination, must have resented her absolute rule in his own palace. He was still alive, after all, a man with a past, a name, a royal tradition of his own. He often went away, to be by himself, to return to his people, their customs, his faith. But then, as soon as he returned to Jezebel, all good intentions vanished.

Elijah, no mean psychologist, must have sensed the turmoil, the doubts, the contained anger inside the king's soul. He took advantage of Jezebel's absence one day to confront the king and provoke him to the duel on Mount Carmel. Being the frustrated ruler he was, Ahab had to accept. The idea appealed to him: the spectacle, the contest, the scope, the risk, the chances, the outcome; this would be the greatest event in contemporary history, with him at the center, at the helm, alone—without Jezebel. Let her see how capable he really was.

We know the outcome. But let us be fair with the king: he was courageous enough—or weak enough —to report fully to his wife. He told her the whole story, about the sacrifices, Elijah's victory, the massacre of her priests, the humiliation of Baal. One can imagine the scene at the royal palace. At this point, we understand everything: Ahab loves Jezebel, who loves Elijah, who is in love with God alone. And God? Whom does He love? This is the question Elijah faces in the desert.

One can visualize Jezebel's rage all the better since it is reported in Scripture. She informed Elijah by messenger: tomorrow you will be dead—tomorrow.

Well, Elijah was too clever, too intelligent not to take her threats seriously; he knew the danger of a woman's fury. He fled into the desert and stayed there forty days and forty nights, and then he had his moving, heartbreaking, and terrifying encounter with God. That encounter remains a high point in the life of the Jewish people—and his own.

Strange: this encounter is marked by despair and not by exuberance. Instead of rejoicing at having defeated Baal and escaping death, Elijah seems dejected, depressed. He wishes to disappear altogether, to die. When God asks him why, he answers: "I have fought for You, I have fought Your children on Your behalf; I have punished those who sinned against You—and now, here I am in a cave, alone, and in danger; I am the last."

Actually, God could have argued with him: "Sad —now? After your triumph?" But arguments never could cure depression. Instead, God chose to tell him a story, which is still a fairly good remedy against melancholy. And God said: "*Tzé*, go, leave the cave and stand upon the mountain before Me." And behold, God passed by, and a great and powerful wind rent the mountains, and broke the rocks into pieces before God; but God was not in the wind. And the wind was followed by an earthquake; but God was not in the earthquake; and the earthquake was followed by a fire; but God was not in the fire; and the fire was followed by a small voice, wrapped in silence. Does that mean that God is in silence? The text does not say so explicitly, but Elijah understood: he wrapped his face in his mantle, went out and stood at the entrance to the cave. And, behold, there came a voice unto him and said: "What are you doing here, Elijah?" And, for the second time, Elijah had to explain: "I fought for You, I alone fought for You—for Your children have forsaken Your covenant, destroyed Your altars, and slain Your prophets with the sword; and now I am left alone, I am in danger too; I am the last."

God's answer is surprising, to say the least. Instead of comforting him, of attenuating his pain and anguish, lifting his spirits, He informs Elijah that his term of office has come to an end. Elisha, son of Shaphat, will be his successor.

Elijah agrees, Elijah always agreed with God. Elijah may even have been pleased. Had not his most fervent wish been to live and die for God—at the hands of God, and not at the hands of the people?

But why did God speak without compassion? How could He remain unmoved by Elijah's outcry that he was alone and the last—the last to recognize the truth, the last to remember, the last to keep so many memories alive?

God spoke without compassion because Elijah had spoken without compassion. Even now he was too harsh with his people. He was angry with the kings for having betrayed their sacred mission by worshipping alien idols. He was angry at the people for having built the wrong altars and for having worshipped false gods. All that is understandable. But the people were not all guilty, as the Midrash emphasizes. Obadiah dared to hide a hundred young prophets, whom Jezebel sought to slaughter. Furthermore, all the neighbors, and the neighbor's neighbors, thus the entire population, knew about them. Yet nobody denounced them to Jezebel. And when Elijah told Jezebel and her husband that he, and he alone, was now serving as God's prophet, everyone knew that this was not so, and nobody spoke up. The Talmud comments: although Ahab's generation was idolatrous, it was equal to David's—for it had no informers.

Elijah's anger seems, therefore, rather excessive. Hence God's response. No one may condemn an entire community. No one, not even its most prestigious prophet, may turn against his own community. He obeyed God's will, but now he must pay the price.

One is not chosen by God without, at the same time, or at one time, becoming His victim.

For having defined himself as being alone—alone against his entire people—Elijah will be admonished by God. This is described in the Midrash more than once. The drought lasted three years because Elijah had predicted it as punishment for the wicked kings and their followers. But what about the children, the innocent? God Himself had to urge Elijah to release Him from His pledge and stop the famine.

At the end, outside the cave, God felt it necessary to plead for His people—against Elijah. Said God: "Why are you so harsh with My people? Are the others better, worthier? Have you seen the pagans at Damascus and elsewhere? Compared to them, My children are good and saintly."

There is irony: God was angry at Elijah for having obeyed Him too well. And so it was time for him to leave and ascend to heaven.

Only to return after having been cast into a totally different role. The post-biblical or post-ascension Elijah has undergone an astonishing metamorphosis. Talmudic legend now represents him as the friend and companion to all those who lack friendship, comfort, and hope. To the cynic, he brings certainty; to the wanderer, a spark of light and warmth. To the sage, a teacher; to the dreamer, a dream: that is Elijah. His visits—or his revelations—are rewards in themselves. One must deserve them.

That is true of his miracles too: they must be deserved. But then, Elijah is reliable, he keeps his promises, fulfills his pledges. And when he is unable to help, at least he suffers with us and weeps over us.

The chastising preacher has become the prophet of consolation. As angel and protector of Israel, he dominates time and space: he is everywhere at the same time. He cannot be described, since his disguises are numerous. Sometimes he appears as an Arab, or a Persian, a Roman, a horseman, a soldier, and even as a woman of questionable trade. On one occasion he had to save Rabbi Meir. Roman soldiers chased him and were about to close in on him when they saw him being picked up by a streetwalker! No, impossible. They turned around and gave up the chase. Clearly, they were second-rate detectives. Why didn't they realize that the woman had to be the prophet Elijah walking with Rabbi Meir in order to save him?

Another story: A certain Rabbi Nahum of Gamzu went on a mission to Rome, bearing Jewish gold, to bribe the emperor into a friendlier attitude towards Judea. On his way he stopped at an inn, where thieves stole his gold and put sand in its place. Imagine the rage of the emperor when he opened the box and found sand. Reb Nahum was sentenced to death for lèse-majesté. *Gam zu letova*, said Reb Nahum, repeating his favorite expression: "whatever is being done is for the best." This time he was right —for Elijah appeared disguised as a courtesan (some say an adviser) and told the emperor: "Wait, this man brought you a precious gift! More precious than gold! His sand has powers; it is a mighty weapon, try it!" He did—and the sand miraculously turned into a weapon capable of destroying the enemy's walls. The emperor rewarded Reb Nahum by offering him a box filled with gold and precious stones. On his way home he stopped in the same inn and was met by the same thieves—who were astonished to see him alive, and rich. They wanted to know what had happened in Rome. He told them. Then they filled ten boxes with the same sand and brought it to the emperor, who used it in battle and saw that it was worthless. And of course, the thieves were jailed, condemned, and hanged. Why didn't Elijah intercede on their behalf too? He was a just man after all. He could have done so, but did not.

He saved another sage—Rabbi Kahana—in a more direct manner. This sage was so poor that he made his living peddling baskets from door to door. His principal customers were women. One of them, a Roman matrona, was so impressed by his beauty that she did what she could to seduce him. He resisted and resisted—but she was stronger. Finally he said: "Let me go and get ready." Instead, he climbed up to the roof and threw himself down. Elijah caught him in midair, saying reproachfully: "Because of you I had to hurry; I was far away." "I had no choice," explained Rabbi Kahana. "I am poor, I am a peddler, I am exposed to all kinds of women, all kinds of dangers." And so, to save him from future similar dangers, Elijah gave him a potful of coins—so that he could give up his peddling career.

But of course Elijah is swifter and a thousand times more passionate when it comes to safeguarding a Jewish community than just an individual. Example: When God chose to allow Haman to annihilate the Jews of Persia, the Torah, dressed like a widow, wept before God, and the angels wept before God, and all said: "If Israel is destroyed, of what use are we in this world?" When the sun and the moon heard the weeping, they withheld their light and Elijah hastened to alert Abraham and Isaac and Jacob and Moses: "Your children are threatened and you are asleep? The angels are weeping, the planets are crying, and you are asleep?" Elijah thus managed to awaken them all and avert disaster.

He could always be counted on to protect the victims, to confound the wicked, to redress injustices and prevent catastrophes. His talents were many: political, economic, even medical. When Rabbi Shimi bar Ashi was bitten by a snake, it was Elijah who cured him. When Rabbi Yehuda ha-Nassi suffered from severe toothaches, he was cured by dentist Elijah.

But the miracle-maker is also a carrier of secrets. Mystics love him: he enriches their quest and their dreams. This is true of some rationalists as well. When two theses are in total contradiction, it is up to Elijah to break the deadlock. One day he will come and resolve all tensions, all conflicts. Arbiter, judge, he possesses the knowledge capable of imposing truth.

Much emphasis is placed on the secret knowledge he communicates to the chosen few. There is even a book attributed to him—*Tana d'bei Eliyahu*—containing his presumed teachings at a school bearing his name.

Often we meet him in the role of human link

between heaven and man, between man and himself. Questions are put to him relating to mysteries that are bound to remain intact. He and he alone could lift the veil and penetrate invisible sanctuaries.

A story: Rabbi Barouka of Huzza visited the market of Lapet. One day Elijah appeared to him there, and Rabbi Barouka asked him: "Is there among the many people here anyone destined to share in the world-to-come?" "There is none," replied Elijah. In the meantime there appeared a man who wore black shoes, but no *Tziziot*—no fringes—on his garment. "This man," remarked Elijah, "this man will share." Thereupon, Rabbi Barouka addressed the stranger and asked him what his occupation was. "I am a jailer," said the stranger. "At night I place my bed between men and women to keep them separate and away from sin." — "And why do you wear black shoes? — "Because I mourn for Jerusalem." — "And why don't you wear *Tziziot?*" — "Because I don't want to be recognized as a Jew. You see, when our rulers plot against our people, I listen and warn our rabbis so that they may pray and avert the menace." Then two other men appeared at the market. "These men too," said Elijah to Rabbi Barouka, "they too will share in the world-to-come." — "What is your occupation?" Rabbi Barouka asked them. — "We are jesters; when we see someone sad, we cheer him up; when people quarrel, we make them laugh."

Elijah is always the one who sees farther, who understands better, and feels deeper. He knows both the right questions and the right answers: when will redemption come? What is the meaning of human suffering? And this one: what does God do while we go on hoping or losing hope in Him, because of Him?

A story: In a talmudic academy a violent debate flared up on a certain issue, and Rabbi Eliezer used all possible arguments to convince his peers but did not prevail. Since reason failed him, he suddenly said: "If I am right, may this carob tree move a hundred yards away." And it did. Not impressed, his colleagues said: "A tree cannot be proof." So Rabbi Eliezer exclaimed: "May the river prove it." And it did: its waters began to flow backwards. Unimpressed, his colleagues shrugged: "Rivers may flow any way they choose, but that has nothing to do with our discussion." "All right, said Rabbi Eliezer, "if I am right, let the walls of this house prove it." And they did; they bent inwards, ready to fall. But Rabbi Joshua rebuked them: "When scholars argue, it is no concern of yours!" So, to please Rabbi Joshua, the walls did not fall down, but to please Rabbi Eliezer, they did not straighten out again. At the end of his wits, Rabbi Eliezer exclaimed: "If I am right, let the heavens prove it." And a heavenly voice was heard saying: "Why are you against my son, Rabbi Eliezer, today? Don't you know that the Law is always as he interprets it?" Finally, they were impressed. Still, Rabbi Joshua jumped to his feet and declared: "The Law is not in heaven—we pay no attention to its voices. Here we go after the majority view."

Later, Rabbi Nathan met Elijah and asked him: "What did God do during the debate? And Elijah smiled and replied: "God listened, and laughed and laughed, saying: *Nitzchuni banai* — 'My children have defeated me."

(As for myself, I would prefer to change the punctuation: *Natzchuni banai.* "Please, children, defeat Me!" God loves to be defeated by His children—but only in debates.)

Once Elijah punished Rabbi Joshua ben Levi by avoiding him. The reason? Because of the following episode. A certain Ulla ben Kosheb was sought by the police; he fled and Rabbi Joshua ben Levi gave him shelter. The police then warned the inhabitants of Lud: "Unless we get him, we'll get all of you." Whereupon Rabbi Joshua ben Levi prevailed upon the fugitive to give himself up. And that is why the prophet was angry.

Actually, he was wrong and the scholar was right. The law of extradition is clear: if a band of heathens surrounds a Jewish community and says, "Give me one of yours and we will kill him, otherwise we shall kill you," the community must resist. Better to be killed than hand over one of its members. But if the heathens mention the fugitive by name, then he is to be handed over. In this case, since the police wanted Ulla ben Kosheb, Rabbi Joshua ben Levi had to extradite him in order to save the community. Why then was Elijah angry? He himself explained: "You are right—but I still don't like informers.

This moved some sages to criticize him for severity and hypersensitivity, as Rabbi José did publicly.

As a result, Elijah snubbed him for a long time. When they met again, Rabbi José said: "Didn't I tell you? You are too sensitive."

But sages and saints are not the only ones to be visited by Elijah. They alone are privileged to see him, but he sees everybody. He loves poor people, pious people, simple people. "God looked about among all the qualities to bestow upon Israel and found none better than . . . poverty," he once declared. He visits all Jewish homes at least once a year —during the Passover Seder service—and attends all circumcision ceremonies. Any Jew entering Jewish society must be welcomed by him; he is present in our joy, as we are present to him.

But he attains his apogee in mystical and Hasidic literature, where he is both master and messenger, source and vessel, form and substance. *Gilui Eliyahu* is more than a concept; it is an adventure close to the Messianic one. Lurianic scholars evoke him in ecstasy. The Besht's companions dedicate their dreams to him. Of all the prophets, it is Elijah who sets the imagination on fire. Why? Because Malachi links him irrevocably to the Messiah? Because of the expression *Veheshiv lev avot al banim* — "he will reconcile children and their parents"? Because he sent a letter to Yehoram ben Yehoshafat seven years after his death? Why has he, of all the prophets, become the symbol of consolation? Why Elijah and not Jeremiah, nor Isaiah? Why has his legend left such an imprint on our mystical quest throughout the generations from and into exile, from and to Jerusalem? Elijah: the great hero, the romantic rescuer, the personification of chivalry, faith, and courage, especially in midrashic and Hasidic tales.

In that literature we are struck by a strange factor: whenever a stranger appears, he takes on the identity of Elijah. At first Elijah is unknown, then the unkown becomes Elijah. A stranger utters a true word, performs a true deed: it must be Elijah. A man with no name or trade emerges from nowhere to accomplish a secret mission: it must be Elijah. The best proof is that he disappears as soon as his work is completed. And his disappearance is as mysterious as his appearance. He responds to our inner need: he is the tenth man for the Minyan, the secret emissary who advises the prince to revoke his evil decree, the compassionate Gentile who stops the hangman at the last minute, the mysterious traveler who arrives at the right moment, at the right place, to prove to a despairing person or a despairing community that hope is forever possible and it has an ever-changing face.

But one day he will come and stay. On that day he will accompany the Messiah, with whose destiny he is linked. One cannot fulfill his mission without the other. For the Messiah to come, he must be preceded—and announced—by Elijah.

In the meantime, he consoles, and occasionally cures, the sick. He encourages the helpless. He takes risks and defies enemies to safeguard Jewish survival: we have no better defender in heaven than Elijah. He is linked to Jewish suffering and speaks about it to God. In fact, he is the chronicler, the historian of

Jewish suffering. He takes note of every tragic event, every massacre, every pogrom, every agony, every tear; thanks to him, nothing is lost. His most magnificent role is that of witness; he is the memory of the Jewish people. Legend has it that at the end of time, his book will become the new Torah which the Messiah will study and teach so that forever afterwards mankind will remember Jewish suffering, Jewish waiting, Jewish longing.

We are back to our initial question: how is one to explain this metamorphosis? How did the prophet of anger become the bearer of promise?

We could try logic and say that one role is the result of the other; because God had wanted him to be severe, unyielding, and pitiless, he subsequently was rewarded by being allowed to symbolize the opposite. This hypothesis is supported by his unique way of dying: he did not actually die, he only ascended to heaven in a chariot of fire, and therefore he—and he alone—can be, and is, still among the living, though in a different role.

But upon rereading the sources one arrives at a less revolutionary explanation. One finds absolutely no contradiction between the biblical and the postbiblical Elijah.

He was kind and charitable even in the beginning, in the biblical tale. He also was severe, but only with kings, rulers, and tyrants, never with the humble, the widows, orphans, and the poor. During the drought, he was sad—*Vayichbosh panav*—he buried his face in sadness; not being able to bear the pain of his people, he caused the rain to come.

He was cruel too, with Jezebel and her court-prophets, but he was tender with the sick child. He killed the false prophets but did not rejoice in their death.

The same is true of Elijah's post-biblical legend: even there he is not entirely forgiving or entirely forbidding; his likes and dislikes remain strong. But when he approves, he does so with his whole being; when he objects, he objects with his whole being. The last act he will have to perform is to kill death. True, he must kill, but his victim will be death itself.

If we return to the beginning of our tale, when Elijah and his young friend walk together for the last time, we can find all the clues necessary to explain why Elijah has captured our imagination.

The prophet is capable of passion, compassion, and friendship. When he is ordered by God to anoint new kings in Israel and outside of Israel, in Aram, and to appoint Elisha as his successor, his heart is heavy with doubt and pain.

Vayelekh misham, says the text. Elijah leaves and finds Elisha plowing the fields. Without a word, Elijah throws him his mantle. Elisha understands the meaning of the gesture, and runs to him, leaving the oxen unattended. "Let me go bid my parents farewell," says Elisha, "then I shall follow you." "What have I told you?" asks Elijah. Or, in other words, "Have you grasped, really grasped, the significance of my gesture, the meaning of our encounter? If so, you no longer belong to your old circle, you no longer are bound by old loyalties. Follow me and me alone." And Elisha followed him, and they were alone.

This poignant exchange permits us to understand the mode of prophecy, its style and bearing. A prophet uses the same words as anyone else, and yet, on his lips, they take on a different meaning. A prophet can discern timeless drama in everyday anecdotes and futile episodes. Thanks to the prophet, time becomes biblical, privileged.

And now we understand Elijah's parting words to Elisha: *You want your powers to be twice as great as mine? If you see me go away, if you know how to look, how to participate in all events, if you know how to face pain and despair and go beyond them, and if later you will be capable of telling about them, your wish will be granted: you will have my powers and yours as well.*

And you will need them. I am your master but you are the survivor. I thought I was alone, and I was—and still am—but now you are with me and you too will be alone, you already are. You will speak and you will need great strength and good fortune to make yourself heard. You will tell people what you have seen, what you have lived—and what I have seen and endured—and you will tell of my departure, you will describe my destiny and how it became flame, you will tell of the fire that has carried me away from you, and the others will refuse to believe you. And I feel sorry for you. You will speak and few will listen, fewer will understand, and still fewer will agree. I feel sorry for you, Elisha, my young friend—

for what you are seeing now, no one will ever see.

And yet, the fire that will carry me away will not stay with me; it will stay with you. Forever.

Saul

This is the story of a journey filled with melancholy, solitude, and anguish. It is a heartbreaking story dealing with all the elements and themes that make up the fabric of life and literature: prophecy and madness, friendship and betrayal, jealousy and acceptance, military adventure and secular ambition, poetry and thirst for power; it even deals with political science and the occult.

There is drama in it, suspense, and action. On many levels, for many reasons.

It is a story filled with awe and passion, inviting compassion; its characters, in constant conflict, are unable to cut themselves away from misfortune—a misfortune that pursues them and which, in a way, they are pursuing with an intensity that ultimately can only crush them.

The isolation of a king, the first and last of a dynasty; the fall of a kingdom, the birth of another; the deterioration of a dream and a friendship: one leaves this tale overwhelmed by grief.

69

Three men walk quietly in the night: the king and his bodyguards, silent shadows moving breathlessly, so as not to make a sound. The enemy, powerful and bent on vengeance, has established camp nearby, at Shunem. To reach En-dor, a hamlet in the foothills of Harei-Ephraim, they must follow a narrow path bordering the Philistine encampment. The smallest carelessness, the simplest error, could be fatal.

After several hours, the three reach their destination. En-dor, huddled in darkness, is asleep, its houses blind; the village is motionless, lifeless.

Still, the three visitors manage to find their way around. Perhaps the king's companions are familiar with the place. One of them knows the person the king wishes to meet: the local sorceress, one of the last witches to remain alive, for the king has massacred most of them.

The king wants her to put him in touch with a dead man. She asks: "What man?" Still incognito, the king answers: "Shmuel—Samuel." She works her magic and, sure enough, here is Samuel, back from the other side, from the world of the dead.

Only now does the witch recognize the king. She is frightened, but he reassures her. Nothing will happen to her; she is safe. But he, the king, is far from being reassured. How could he be? Samuel, the prophet, speaks to him in anger: "Why did you disturb my peace?" "I need you," says the unhappy king. "I need help. I am going to war tomorrow without knowing whether God is with me or against me. I am afraid. Help me; you can, you alone can help.

Tell me God's will—only you can do that, since God refuses to speak to me or even notice my presence. I don't exist for Him. You, the prophet and defender of God's first king, you must come to my aid."

But Samuel, from beyond death, refuses, and continues speaking to him angrily: "You want my help? Now? First you deny God's word, ridicule God's command—and now you wish to be helped? You are lost, and it is time you realized it. Your enemies will defeat you in battle; you will perish, and worse: your kingdom will perish with you. Another man will follow you, succeed you as King of Israel—and his House will not be destroyed, ever."

The prophet withdraws, leaving King Saul crushed by despair, unable to speak, to cry, to move, to protest, to scream, to throw his pain and anguish into the face of history, into the night which, outside, grows more and more menacing. He wants to return to his headquarters, to his home. But he feels weak. The witch feels sorry for him and offers him a meal. "Eat," she says, "it will do you good." Indifferent, proud, he rejects her pity.

We now leave the occult, and the scene becomes realistic, almost grotesque: his two companions join the sorceress in insisting that he eat—until he gives in. And there Saul, once a mighty and glorious king, partakes of his last meal. Then he leaves, to return to his camp, where his sons, lieutenants, and soldiers are awaiting him. He walks slowly, slower than before, lost in thought: he is living his last night and is aware of it. He will not be able to count on anyone for his ultimate battle. It will all be over for him and his allies—tomorrow. He knows it, and goes towards death alone. The king, anointed by God, is alone like God—and like Him, silent.

How are we to understand Saul's strange nocturnal visit to En-dor. Did he want to see Samuel again in order to come closer to God once more? Didn't he know that the way to God does not lead through the violation of His laws? Didn't he understand that, by soliciting the witch's help, he only increased the distance separating him from his only source of salvation? Did he really think that Samuel, prophet and priest, messenger of God, would address him in a language other than that of anger? Or was he desperate? And if so, was it the fault of men who had abandoned him, or of God who had rejected him? If God was the cause of his desperation, why didn't Saul turn to Him directly, without intermediaries? Could it be that he came to Samuel fully aware of the futility of his action? Could it be that he knew that nothing could or would change after their meeting? Is it possible that he came to En-dor in order to be defeated, to be humiliated again? To attract Samuel's anger and the old witch's pity? To illustrate and accelerate his downfall? To bring to a climax the process of self-destruction?

These are but of few of the disturbing questions that confront us when we explore the life and career of King Saul. There are many more, and some will necessarily remain unanswered. Even so, the questions themselves can lead to a better understanding of an extraordinary man—extraordinary because of the problems he raises and the events he recalls. He is both pathetic and mysterious, disquieting and human, profoundly human—even in his failures.

The principal characters in the cast? Samuel: judge and prophet. Saul: prophet and king. David: king and poet. Immediately, we are conquered by Saul. Majestic and humble at the same time, he inspires sympathy and commands respect. After his coronation, he does not settle in a luxurious palace, nor does he develop a taste for praise and glory. He works like everyone else, behaves like everyone else, and uses his position to strengthen the security of his country. Having accepted Samuel's constitution, he installs a state council with ministers and officers, and transforms every village into a fortress, every citizen into a fighter.

When Nahash, king of the Ammonites, launches an attack across the Jordan against the tribes in Gilead, Saul calls for collective action. He orders a yoke of oxen to be cut into pieces and sent to the neighboring regions with a warning that the same will be done to the oxen of anyone who will not follow Samuel and Saul. And everyone understands, and follows.

Israel's political history begins with Saul, and under his rule becomes a power to be reckoned with.

But then, why was he pushed into degradation? Why did his kingdom end with him? Why was he condemned to live with a past but denied a future? Because he offended Samuel's sensibilities? Because he wished to spare the life of Agag, king of the Amalekites? Or because he visited the old witch at En-dor? Simply because God changed His mind and suddenly preferred David? Saul was a good and faithful man caused by God to leave his father's house. Saul had never dreamed of becoming king, had never aspired to rule over anyone; he had been chosen by God for a task that he did not seek. Why then was he slandered, judged, punished? Did God draw him closer only to strike him harder?

No wonder he captured the fancy of great poets, painters, composers. Rembrandt and Holbein, Byron and Rilke, Lamartine, Handel, D. H. Lawrence, and André Gide were all inspired by the tragic nobility, the romantic gravity of his singular yet exemplary destiny. More than any king who followed, Saul has intrigued creative spirits. Even more than David, whose impact was greater both historically and metaphysically, Saul attracts anyone who approaches Judaism from esthetic and ethical viewpoints. David and his conquests make us proud, but it is Saul and his failures that fascinate us. More complex than David, more tormented and tortured, Saul lifts us to mountain heights and then drops us into the abyss. Few personalities experienced as many metamorphoses, dramas, or breakdowns as Saul; few destinies ever followed as fast a rhythm, or had as many vicissitudes in rapid succession. Few men knew such glory, and few lost it for such absurd reasons.

Saul: a flame caught in the tempest. A story of

solitude, a beautiful adventure turned sour, or, as André Neher, in his perceptive analysis of the man, calls it: an *acte manqué*. Saul: a story of misplaced pity.

The narrative opens with a rather banal episode about mules who, by accident, without explanation, have gone astray somewhere in the fields. Their owner, a man of the tribe of Benjamin, sends his son Saul to recover them, but without success. Instead, Saul meets Samuel, who tells him, without any preparation or introduction, that he will be king.

Suddenly, Saul changes: he becomes another person, as the text says with great emphasis: *venihye leish acher*. Falling under the influence of Samuel, he turns into an emissary of God, a man above men, a man with a secret. Marked by destiny, he becomes part of the chosen class. From that moment, he no longer expresses himself as before, in terms of daily work and sustenance. He forgets his mules, his mind is elsewhere, his soul in turmoil. He joins a group of wandering prophets and adopts their bizarre behavior. Singing and dancing and shouting, he takes part in their services, with ectasy. His former friends, astonished, wonder aloud: "What? Saul—a prophet?" It seems peculiar, incredible, impossible. His uncle questions him: "All this is very fine, very entertaining, but what about the mules? Where are the mules?" And Saul must descend from the lofty level of spiritual discovery to earthly matters. To speak about . . . mules. "Don't worry," he says, "they have been found." That is all he says. He does not reveal the great change that has occurred in him, a change that instantly turns the poor shepherd that he was, into a king. He withholds his secret. Not even his prophet friends are informed.

The fact that his having joined the prophets provokes such surprise, means that he does not fit the part; he neither looks nor behaves like a prophet. He is neither particularly pious nor learned, observant, wise, nor ascetic. What then is he?

Actually, the Bible describes him as young, handsome, good-hearted, and tall: head and shoulders above all men in Israel. He is virtuous and shy, as are many giants who find their physical strength somewhat cumbersome. He is a good son, who listens to his father and obeys his orders without question. For three days he looks for the lost mules—because his father asked him to do so. His visit to Samuel is his father's idea; Saul himself would not have taken the initiative. And when that prophet mentions something about his being destined for royalty, Saul answers modestly that he does not deserve such an honor—and that his father is waiting for him ... and the mules.

The Midrash describes him more poetically, more artistically—and less realistically. He is pure, and "innocent like a one-year-old baby." Devoted to his people, loyal to God, brave and always ready for battle in the name of Israel and the God of Israel, an excellent Jew and valiant soldier, he observes the religious precepts even while in military service. Strangely, the Midrash seems to prefer him to David. It says that David has many wives; Saul, only one. David marches behind his troops, while Saul leads them into battle. David loves to take; Saul, to give. After defeating Amalek, Saul divides the loot and gives one sheep to each of his 200,000 soldiers. David has troubles with his children, not so Saul.

Is Saul really as the Midrash calls him, *Bekhir adoshem*, God's chosen? Yes and no. Samuel, and beyond him, God, does not want Saul to be king for the simple reason that they want no king at all. God and God alone is the King of Israel. And Israel must serve Him and Him alone. Him—and not capricious, vain, arrogant, cruel, and mortal tyrants. Samuel says so explicitly: "And the elders of Israel asked Samuel to appoint for us a king to govern us like all the nations." Samuel, the supreme judge, outspoken and perceptive, tries to dissuade them, warning: "The king will exploit you, he will use your men as soldiers, your women as servants." But his arguments fall on deaf ears; they hold to their idea, they want a king, they want to be like other nations. So it is for lack of a better solution that Samuel—acting for God—grants their wish and chooses Saul, who, characteristically, is neither judge nor priest nor prophet, as though to stress the point that since there must be a king, he should come from the people and remain attached to them.

Here Saul enters a new phase: he no longer belongs to his family or tribe alone, but to the entire people of Israel. Designated and anointed secretly by Samuel, he is to be elected, crowned—or confirmed in his election—by all the tribes meeting in plenary session at Mizpah.

It is worth noting that, at first, Saul tries to hide. Is it a game? Instead of calling him by name, Samuel makes all the men of all the tribes march by, and as they file past him, he looks at them in silence. Finally, they realize that one man is missing—and Saul is found amidst the baggage. "He is the one," says Samuel, "he is your king." And the people shout: "Long live the king." And "Samuel told the people the manner of the kingdom and wrote it in a book." It is the first constitutional document in history, stipulating the obligations as well as the privileges of a king with regard to his subjects. Then Samuel sends everybody home—including Saul, even though he is king. King against his will, he returns to his routine. And the text does not hesitate to admit that, right away, there are among Saul's new subjects those who whisper their discontent. Yet he says nothing, and Samuel, who also hears them, says nothing. King Saul's reign thus begins in conflict.

His first problem is with Samuel—an impersonal conflict between spiritual and secular authorities, between the prophet and the ruler. The prophet wishes to interfere in the nation's political and social affairs and, naturally, the king opposes him. Saul maintains a kind of sovereignty but cannot ignore Samuel's towering figure that stands behind him, as though to watch him, guide him and supervise him. Whether the king wants it or not, he cannot do anything without consulting the prophet, who now serves as his principal mentor and conscience.

Does it please him? Does it bother him? Perhaps both. Does it sound paradoxical? Saul remains a living contradiction in all he does. On one hand he resents Samuel's authority, but on the other he needs him. Whenever the prophet is away, the king feels lost, insecure. He wants nothing more than to share his powers with God's representative. Just imagine: he goes so far as to disturb Samuel's eternal peace, to obtain his advice and help. He cannot function without him—and that troubles him.

His ambivalent feelings towards Samuel are further complicated by other elements in their relationship. Saul knows that he owes Samuel a great deal, if not everything. Does he resent him for reminding him of that debt? Then too, Saul knows perfectly well that Samuel is against monarchy. A matter of principle? Surely. Still, Saul, subconsciously, can entertain some doubts in this respect. How can he be sure that Samuel's opposition is not personally motivated?

We must not forget that the emergence of royalty is linked to the extinction of the institution of judges, of whom Samuel was the last. His own two sons, Joel and Abiah, were shown little respect because they did not resemble their father. Although they served as local judges, it is believed that they yielded to corruption. Instead of going to the people, as their father had done, they let people—the wrong ones—come to them. That was why they could not succeed their father, and why Samuel had to allow Saul to take over. Thus, the judge could have felt bitterness towards the king—or, at least, the king might have thought he did. Hence, Saul's mixed feelings towards Samuel throughout his entire life.

But then, that was true also of his relationships with the other individuals around him: his favorite singer, David; his daughter, Michal; his son, Jonathan; and even . . . God.

To understand this strange, though oddly appealing character, let us examine the setting and context of his dramatic career.

We are in the middle of the tenth century, B.C.E. Besieged, oppressed by its neighbors, the people of Israel suffer from internal divisions along tribal lines. Everyone fights for his own ground, his own aims, and is indifferent to the fate of the others. The enemy is powerful and ruthless—and omnipresent. Its armies are numerous: the Edomites, the Moabites, Arameans, Ammonites, Amalekites. The beaten, humiliated people of Israel no longer possess the necessary iron for the fabrication of swords, the Philistines have taken it all, as they have taken the *Aron habrit*, the sanctuary holding Judaism's most sacred writings. Disarmed, Israel; vanquished, God's people, the people who are supposed to bear witness to God's glory and eternity. Fear and resignation are everywhere. Then one day, King Nahash of Ammon tells the inhabitants of Jabesh-Gilead that if they capitulate, they will be allowed to remain alive—but each with only one eye. To ridicule and frighten them even more, he tells them: "Go and run, run seven days in any direction, and try to find refuge with any people; we shall catch you and we shall see you on your knees."

In their despair, the inhabitants of Jabesh-Gilead send an appeal to Saul. Would he come to their rescue? He accepts the challenge, organizes a retaliatory action, and saves the honor of Israel, thus justifying the hopes history has placed in him. Saul: military leader, commander and protector of his nation, defender of its name. Saul: judge, teacher, king—a mixture of Samson, Samuel, and David. He is the first to impose the principle of national unity and national defense upon his dispersed people; the first to view events in their historical perspective; the first to invoke solidarity as a national duty: whenever a part, a fragment, of the nation is assaulted, all must react. Under his reign, the people of Israel become one, not only spiritually, but physically and militarily as well.

Chosen to wage war, Saul can no longer find peace; until his last day he fights the enemies of his people—enough of them always remain to provoke him. Hardly does the southern front quiet down than the one in the North flares up. Neither Israel nor her enemies ever wins a definitive victory. As a result, there is constant uncertainty everywhere, a sense of collective and individual insecurity. The king himself is affected by it. He grows moody, suspicious, temperamental, even in his private life. Just as he suspects enemies on the borders, he suspects plots in his immediate entourage. Poor king, he has, after all, no royal tradition or inherited experience to fall back on; he does not know how kings should behave; beleaguered king, he needs a mentor to teach him what to do, what to say, when and where. One day, wanting to assert his inner independence, he decides not to wait for Samuel but to start sacrificial ceremonies without him. Samuel, of course, flies into a rage and predicts his punishment then and there: the House of Saul is bound to fall. Saul understands that he never will be able to free himself from his private and national tutor. And this realization must have hurt as much as the prediction about the future of his kingdom.

He becomes melancholy, sad, withdrawn, subject to fits of anger and depression. From time to time he follows strange impulses. For instance, he massacres all the priests of Nob and all those allegedly endowed with occult powers—in other words, all those beyond his royal authority, all who reminded him of his own limitations.

Then, to make things worse, a new hero appears in his life and in the life of his people: David, a man as brave and as handsome as Saul, and also chosen by God to reign over his people—the same people. Saul loves and hates him—for the same reasons: for his intelligence, his courage, his poetic sense, his musical abilities, and loyalty. David is what Saul once was—and more so: he is what Saul would like to be.

As soon as David arrives on the scene, he steals the show. Goliath defies Saul, but it is David who responds to the challenge and defeats him. It is David's singing voice alone which can disperse the darkness in Saul. Just as Samuel dispels his doubts,

David disarms his sadness. And again, as with Samuel, Saul needs David's presence. Surely, at one point, he must resent it; he must realize how dependent on David he is. As with Samuel, Saul becomes aware of how insecure he is in this relationship as well. The king is king, but he is not sovereign.

Saul resents David even more deeply than he does Samuel. The prophet is severe—and unhappy though he may be, the king understands why. But David is gracious, helpful, and kind, always kind, almost to the point of annoyance, and Saul cannot understand why David is so attached, so devoted. What can the young man want, what is he after? He must have a reason, a motive . . . Saul simply cannot believe that David's attachment to him is genuine, disinterested. To play it safe, the king tries to have him marry his eldest daughter. David declines the offer, as though to stress that he expects no reward for his services—and this confuses Saul even more. Finally, he makes another attempt and offers his youngest daughter, Michal. Was she prettier than her sister, or was David in a more conciliatory mood? Or did he think it impolite to offend a king—and a father —twice? In any case, he accepts the offer of marriage with Michal.

Now it would seem natural for David to serve his father-in-law. And Saul, therefore, should no longer find it disconcerting. But he remains suspicious. He feels that David hovers over him too much, and does not spend enough time with his wife, Michal. When David is not with him, Saul wonders where he is,

83

what he is doing, and with whom he is plotting. Saul becomes increasingly convinced that David is seeking to seize power and replace him on the throne. And yet, he needs him. And so, to help himself overcome this inner need to listen to David's melodious voice, the need to be entertained by his words, Saul feels compelled to persecute, torment, and punish him. He is even ready to kill him, not having learned Machiavelli's lesson that political assassinations are doomed to be senseless; no king has ever managed to kill his successor. But then, Saul, in this respect, is acting irrationally: he hates David because he loves him; he wants to eliminate him because he is under his spell. Saul wants to kill to be free—free from David, from his love for David. More than once, David's life is in danger; he is always saved by Michal and her brother Jonathan, who act as his informers. Whenever Saul's mood turns threatening, they warn David and help him flee. As a result, Saul's rage acquires new force; it is boundless: the whole world, his own children included, is against him.

Despite or because of his complexity, Saul seems profoundly pathetic: one cannot but empathize with his fate. His sadness is neither paranoia nor delusion; it is rooted in reality. And we understand his anger. Remember that it was he who militarily and psychologically prepared his nation for battle and victory, yet it is David who triumphs. Worse: David is praised at Saul's expense; when compared to the old king, of course the young warrior comes out ahead. What does the man in the street say? That Saul killed the enemy by the thousands, but David did it by the tens of thousands! Why such gratuitous analogies from an ungrateful nation? Why can the people not applaud David without hurting the old king? Why does Samuel, in his position as prophet and God's spokesman, go as far as anointing David in secret, behind the king's back? No wonder that Saul is enraged and feels the urge to rid himself of the young usurper. What can he think but that David has intentionally, deliberately, deceitfully come close to him, allegedly to help and entertain, when in reality, he wants to steal his crown and kingdom! Having reached such conclusions, how else can the king behave? Should he shrug his shoulders and accept his fate with equanimity? Impossible! The more he thinks of David, the more he feels he unmasks his shrewdness and opportunism. Not only does David prove to be a masterful manipulator and politician, but he also manages to alienate from Saul the affection of all the people dearest to him: first Samuel, then Michal and Jonathan! How can one not feel sympathy for Saul, the most tragic and lonely of kings? How can one not take his side? Inevitably, at this point, one feels closer to him than to David.

Especially since David's behavior during the last phase of Saul's reign strikes us as singularly unethical. Saul's suspicions and personal animosity put aside, where is David when Saul readies himself and his army to face the enemy in their final confrontation? Where he should not be—on the enemy's side, in one of its fortresses, Ziklag, where he has pledged to remain neutral. Imagine: here are Jewish soldiers going to war to defend their homes and their honor, and David does not join them. Is he going to stand aside and watch while Jews might be killed by the hundreds? The nation is in danger, Israel can suffer shame and defeat—and David is to remain an onlooker? Doesn't he know that in conflict, neutrality is sinful and it helps the aggressor? But then, given this situation, upon whom can Saul rely? Granted, David fled to Ziklag to escape Saul's vengeful wrath, but this is war! Why doesn't he return to lead his troops? Saul needs him more than ever—he would receive him with honors! Does David stay at Ziklag out of fear, or weakness? But then, if a hero like David weakens, how can Saul count on the resolve of his officers and their men? Small wonder then that, several hours before the attack, Saul needs to talk to someone . . . albeit a witch! Betrayed by his allies, abandoned by his friends, rejected by God, where else can he turn?

God is against him, and Saul knows it: hadn't Samuel said so again and again? The final break came during the unfortunate episode with the Amalekite king Agag. Yes, Saul disobeyed Samuel and refused to execute his royal adversary; yes he gave in to his feelings, his compassion, and is his own victim. Is that a reason to condemn him irrevocably? Yes, says Samuel, because Saul is too kind, too charitable; because he is unwilling to behead a human being, be it his enemy, he is doomed to lose his kingdom. Between the voices of heaven and his heart, he chooses to listen to his heart. But then, in our eyes, his sin cannot but make him more attractive. If nobility and compassion be a sin, how can one dislike the sinner?

Saul's humanism is emphasized and treated with deep understanding in midrashic literature. We are told he refused to kill not only Agag but also the civilians among the Amalekites and their animals. Contrary to Samuel's strict orders, he argued as follows: does not the Torah prohibit the slaughter of an animal and her young on the same day? How then, he argued, could I kill parents and children together? And, he went on to say: "Even if men have sinned, wherein lies the guilt of animals? Even if the adults have committed crimes, what have the children done?"

How can one not love Saul for these questions? One wonders whether he expected an answer. Well, he did get one, but not from Samuel, who must have found it difficult to refute such arguments. The answer came directly from a *Bat-kol*, a heavenly voice, that admonished him: "Do not overdo things—do not be more just than necessary." An excess of charity may be sinful. Nonetheless, he refused to kill.

That was his mistake, says the Midrash. For Haman was to be Agag's descendant, which means that Saul is responsible for Haman's later massacre of Jews. Or, as Resh-Lakish put it: "Whoever chooses to show pity to a cruel person will in the end be cruel to men capable of pity." It is all a question of timing: misplaced pity is potentially no less dangerous than unwarranted cruelty. And that is why Saul deserved to be punished.

Still, we are moved by his humaneness. Between
a king who is too cruel and one not cruel enough,
we prefer the latter. Saul, after all, never sought to
occupy a position where he would have to kill. God
compelled him to accept it—without ever telling him
that royalty, or authority, also involves the shedding
of blood. Couldn't he turn to God and say: "Tell me,
Master of the Universe, why did You lift me so high
if You meant to push me down later? Why did You
choose to make me king—only to repudiate me later
—and for what reason? For not being able to kill a
human being, just like that, face to face? You knew
from the beginning that David would be king, and
that his line, not mine, would last forever. Why did
You need me? Why did You make a fool, an executioner out of me? Why did You make me play a part
on David's stage without telling me that it was only
a game?

King against his will, hero or anti-hero against
his will, Saul went to see the witch, not in order to
find Samuel and God, but to inform them of his
break with them. The play was over.

The final act is sheer drama. Left alone, alone
with his sons and soldiers, alone with his desperate
truth, he goes into battle knowing that all is lost. His
sons are slain, his soldiers beaten. As for himself, he
begs his arms-bearer to kill him. And, absurdity of
absurdity, the servant refuses to obey because the
plea comes from a king; it is forbidden to lift a
finger against a person anointed by God. Thus, his
election, his royalty works against him to the very

end: were he a simple officer, his servant would obey, but Saul is not a simple man. And so, he falls on his own sword and dies.

Even then, David somehow manages to steal the scene by suddenly appearing to deliver the eulogy for both Jonathan, his best friend, and the king: "The beauty of Israel is slain upon Thy high places; oh, how are the mighty fallen.... Saul and Jonathan were lovely and pleasant in their lives, and in their death they were not divided: they were swifter than eagles, stronger than lions . . . oh, how are the mighty fallen."

This lamentation is poignant, majestic, and lyrical. But, in the Midrash, David is reprimanded by God: "What? Saul has fallen and you feel like singing?"

No. Of the two, David has the less appealing role. We weep for Saul and withdraw from David. And we disagree with history's choice.

But, in the name of fairness, let us examine the situation from another viewpoint. Let us look more closely at David, and see the relationship through his eyes.

Granted, in his youth he does seem rather aggressive, even pretentious. Nobody asked him—he volunteers to challenge a giant of a warrior; he is at the right place at the right moment, in the right role. Must Goliath be defeated? David will do it. Does Israel need a hero? David. The king needs an analyst? David. Sure of himself, decisive. But then, what should he have done? Nothing? Should he have let

Israel bow before Goliath? Allowed the king to yield to despair? Since no absolutes exist in life, every choice necessarily means compromise. David chooses to ignore appearances; only results count. Only the people and its history are important. He goes everywhere, volunteers for every mission, because he is needed; he alone can do what he does. And when a nation's life is at stake, how can one think of appearances, of what critics may say?

Moreover, David's behavior towards Saul is above reproach. He is respectful, obliging, loyal, and admiring. He never seeks to harm him. Quite the contrary: he only wants to help. He does not wish to succeed the old king, but on the contrary, to keep him healthy and in power. All he wants is to serve and comfort him, to cheer him up. As soon as the king needs him, he is there—even when it means exposing himself to peril or death. Why? Simply because he loves his king; yes, he really loves him—as only a poor shepherd boy can love the sovereign who rescued him from anonymity and poverty and befriended him. David loves Saul with all his heart; he gives him his time and his innocence; he fights for him and his name. And if at first he refuses to marry the king's eldest daughter, it is precisely to prove to him how pure his love for the king is—untainted, disinterested, and selfless.

Saul has fits of unjustified violence; David says nothing. Saul persecutes him; he says nothing. Saul makes him into his personal scapegoat; still David remains silent. Saul wants him dead, and David still continues to love him, to worship him. Expelled from the royal quarters, exiled, hunted everywhere, David does not respond in kind. He never seems to have expressed hatred for Saul, or even anger. On three occasions he manages to get inside Saul's tent; on three occasions he has the opportunity to kill him—and is urged by his companions to do so: kill the sick old man, they say, lest his jealousy, his spite, his hate destroy you. But he is not even tempted to do so. David somehow understands that they are both victims. Saul is God's victim, David is Saul's. And it is because of the depth of his understanding that David is given the privilege of conferring an eternal dimension upon his kingdom.

Of course, David is no saint. And Scripture admits it: there is no cover-up in the Bible. His sin with Bathsheba leaves a stain on his name, a blemish on his life. His military operations are praised, but only half-heartedly; he has fought too many battles, shed too much blood. Thus the Temple in his city will be built by his son who symbolizes peace.

Yet, the essential difference between the two kings emerges clearly: Saul signifies internal tension and conflict, while David represents their resolution; it is David, not Saul, who ultimately unifies the people.

Furthermore, Saul lacks the self-assurance necessary to obtain and retain power. He is forever making decisions and regretting them. True, in the Midrash, his motivation for letting Agag's cattle live is idealistic, but not so in Scripture, which claims that he merely wants to appease his soldiers by giving them the enemy loot. Yet, when Samuel questions him about it, Saul does not dare admit the truth. Listen to the text: when the prophet meets the king, the king lies and tells him that he did fulfill God's command to kill the Amalekites and all that belonged to them.

Another difference: Saul is jealous, David is not. Saul is jealous of David's popularity and fame. People praise David more and Saul cannot bear that. And what is the praise all about? Killing. People say: Saul kills thousands, but David tens of thousands. But then, isn't Saul a humanist? Isn't he against capital punishment, against killing? He should be pleased to be known as one who kills only thousands.

Also: in spite of his humanistic language, he has martial tendencies. David's symbol is the harp, Saul's the spear. He always seems to have one in his hand. After promising immunity to the surrendering Gibeonites, he breaks that promise and massacres them—which no king ought do, which no man must do.

Saul is indecisive, unable to handle things by himself. Why does he allow Samuel to serve as intermediary with God? David needs none. Man, as a general rule, can and must address himself to God directly—and this is even truer of kings chosen by God. Saul doubts too much and David not enough. Thus Saul would be an excellent philosopher, but David is a better king.

David punishes his enemies on the outside, while Saul hunts them within. While David fights Philistines, Saul distrusts Jews; Saul goes as far as killing

Jews: What he refused to do unto Amalek, he did to the priests of Nob: he exterminated them all without pity. David fights invaders, Saul his friends. David refuses to kill Saul, the Jewish king, whereas Saul plans to kill David but refuses to kill Agag, the Amalekite king. Saul is ready to liquidate David but cannot, whereas David could have killed Saul on three occasions but did not. That is why David, and not Saul, has been chosen to symbolize Jewish royalty.

True, Saul suffers, but suffering is no excuse. He is wrong to make others suffer. David also suffers, but he uses that suffering to create songs and generate joy.

And yet, having come to concur with history's judgment, we must add that, despite all objective considerations, all reasons of state, Saul continues to move us. There is human beauty as well as weakness in his wounded soul. At times, he appears even more majestic than his successor. A painting by Rembrandt shows him half-hidden behind a curtain, weeping silently, while listening to David's singing accompanied by his harp. He is sad, this first king of Israel, and his sadness has survived him.

If only he had decapitated Agag. That was the real beginning of his fall. Why did he refuse? Was it pity for a fallen king on whom God had vented His wrath? We could have understood that. But again the text prevents us from going too far afield. It has its own explanation. Saul chose not to kill Agag but to chain and torment him, to publicly humiliate him and keep him alive as an eternal prisoner, a reminder of his eternal defeat. And there, we must admit, death itself would seem more humane, more charitable. Agag himself preferred it. Listen to the text: Samuel ordered him brought, "and Agag came unto him in chains. And Agag said: 'Surely the bitterness of death is at hand.' And Samuel said: 'As thy sword has made women childless, so shall thy mother be childless among women.' And Samuel beheaded Agag before the Lord in Gilgal." Agag, visibly, went to his death quietly. For him, death was a liberation from his chains. This Saul did not know.

Misunderstood himself, Saul was incapable of understanding others. He understood no one. He should have been more aware of Samuel's suffering at having to transmit God's word and God's will without being able to change them. He should have tried to understand the conflict of David, who was compelled to replace him though he loved him. Nor did he empathize with his own children, who, out of love for him, tried to stop him from committing the irrevocable. Saul was alone and never managed to go beyond his solitude.

He was alone when he died—and suddenly, in our legend, he is forgiven and even rehabilitated. Look at Saul, says God to His angels. He knows he is going to die, yet he faces death with his eyes open. And better yet: he is taking his sons with him. Why? To not die alone? One always does, anyway. Poor Saul: in his compassion, he spares the life of an enemy king, but that compassion does not extend to a Jewish king, the first in history, the unhappiest as well.

Saul killed Saul. And, strangely enough, his gesture does not surprise us. Suicide means a wish to be at once executioner and victim, mortal creature and Angel of Death. It is a gesture which combines giving and receiving. In life and in death, Saul remains unique.

He brought his tragedy upon himself. He was his own enemy, and though we are all David's subjects, we remain Saul's friends.

Jeremiah

And it came to pass that when Jerusalem was destroyed, God entered the burning sanctuary. He saw it in flames and began to weep. And He said to Jeremiah, who stood nearby: "Why are you not weeping? I am like the father whose only son died on the day of his wedding, during the ceremony. And you, Jeremiah, feel no pain—neither for the father nor the son? Go, go, Jeremiah, go wake the Fathers of My people. Wake up Abraham and Isaac and Jacob. And Moses, wake him too. Tell them I wish to see them. I need them because they know how to weep."

Jeremiah was recalcitrant. "Moses," he argued, "cannot be found since nobody knows where he is buried—nobody but You." "All right," said God. "Go to the banks of the river Jordan and shout: 'Son of Amram, son of Amram, rise and see your children and theirs being slain by their enemies.' Do what I say. He will hear, he will understand; he will come to be with Me."

And so Jeremiah went first to the *Mearat*

Hamakhpela—the cave where Abraham and Isaac and Jacob are resting—and gave them the message that God wanted to see them. "Why?" they asked. "Why on this day of all days?" And the prophet, probably embarrassed by the terrifying content of his message, evaded the question and said: "I do not know," which surely was not true. He knew— of course he knew: God had told him the reason. But he was fearful, says the Midrash. He was afraid the patriarchs would hold him responsible for the catastrophe he had witnessed.

He felt the same apprehension as he addressed Moses, who also wished to know: "What has happened in the world—to the world—that I am suddenly called upon to appear before God?" And again Jeremiah answered: "I do not know."

Moses then turned to the angels, who told him: "Jerusalem is on fire, the Temple is in ruins." In an outburst of anger, Moses cursed the sun: "Why didn't you remain dark and thus prevent the enemy from slaughtering my people?" "I had no choice," said the sun. Having heard his angry words, the three patriarchs turned to him and wondered aloud: "Why are you shouting, Moses?" "You don't know?" he answered. "Aren't you aware of what is happening to our descendants?" And he told them. Whereupon they tore their clothes in mourning. "Why are You punishing Your people?" Abraham asked God. "They have sinned," said God. "They have transgressed against the commandments of the Torah." "I demand proof," said Abraham. "Let the Torah come forth and be My witness," said God.

The Torah made its appearance. But as it was about to speak, Abraham stopped it, saying: "You are forgetting; you are forgetting the day when God offered you to all the nations in the world; all rejected you, all except the nation of Israel; and now, you are about to become its accuser?" So the Torah kept quiet, as did all the other witnesses for the prosecution. And God's deed received no final justification. But it was late, too late to change the past: what had been done could not be undone. Jerusalem was burning; and Jewish children, already in exile, had no more strength left to wander; all they could do was dream.

This poignant legend illustrating the cosmic tragedy within the Jewish catastrophe by linking Jewish suffering across generations and spheres does raise certain questions.

One: Why did God seek the presence of the Jewish forefathers after and not before the catastrophe? Why had they not been informed? The Jewish people were suffering, and they were unaware? Asleep?

Two: God told Jeremiah He wished to see the patriarchs, who know how to weep. Are we to understand that he, Jeremiah, did not? Is it conceivable that Jeremiah, the prophet of collective Jewish suffering, the visionary of fire and blood, the author of Lamentations, did not know how to cry?

Three: Why did Jeremiah fear the patriarchs' criticism? Since when was he afraid of critics? Why would anyone hold him responsible for events that he, throughout his entire life and with all the strength of his being, tried to prevent? Hadn't he devoted long years of work and effort to warning people of oncoming dangers? If there existed a man, one man in Judah, in the world, who could have said to others and himself, "This horror, these massacres are not my doing," it was he. Then why such reticence on his part to confront his forebears? How is one to comprehend his weakness? If anyone had the right to question and pass judgment, it was he. But then why was he afraid to tell the truth and give an authentic report to Abraham and Isaac and Jacob, who, anyway, were reduced to shedding tears at a time when they were already useless?

Jeremiah's contradictions, his constant search for himself in a society which turned away not only from him but from itself, his determined quest for truth in times of falsehood (the very word "falsehood" appears seventy-two times in biblical literature, half of them in the Book of Jeremiah), his doubts, his tears, his yearning for meaning and silence: few personalities possess his richness and even fewer his tragic depth. His lyricism remains unmatched, his scope unparalleled. No one is as appealing or as removed.

Jeremiah was forever torn between God and Israel, Israel and other nations, big powers and smaller powers, between his lost childhood and his unbearable old age. He is perplexing and intriguing; he arouses every passion from extreme hatred to infinite fidelity; he is an outsider and, as such, is misunderstood. He is, in short, a survivor, a witness. Of all the prophets, he alone predicted the catastrophe, experienced it, and lived to tell the tale. He alone sounded the alarm before the fire, and after being singed by its flames went on to retell it to any who would listen. Whenever we are struck by misfortune, we turn to him and follow in his footsteps; we use his words to describe our struggles.

At first, Jeremiah seems simple, even simplistic. He is a weak man who always cries—and always with reason; in fact, he seems to do nothing else. He goes through his life shedding tears.

Only after we study the text and the character do we realize that his simplicity is deceptive. His personality contains puzzling and mystifying aspects. Just imagine: having made us believe for generations that Jeremiah indulged in weeping, we discover in the Midrash, already quoted, that he did not even cry when Jerusalem was destroyed.

Let us read:

"The words of Jeremiah, son of Hilkiah, one of the priests at Anathoth in the territory of Benjamin. The words of the Lord came to him in the days of King Josiah, son of Amon of Judah, in the thirteenth year of his reign, and throughout the days of King Jehoiakim, son of Josiah of Judah, until the end of the eleventh year of King Zedekiah, son of Josiah of Judah, when Jerusalem went into exile in the fifth month. . . ."

As with every genuine work of art, this opening statement contains all that is to follow. From the short biographical notice we already learn much about the character himself and the events surrounding him: an obscure beginning, a dramatic conclusion, and several short-lived royal regimes. And all the rest is prophecy.

"One of the priests at Anathoth ... in the territory of Benjamin." Whoever is familiar with biblical geography understands the implications of these two lines. Poverty and sadness dominate the homes of Benjamin, whose tribe fared the worst of all the twelve tribes during the partition of the land under Joshua. Their territory was narrow and long and dry: no fields, no trees, no fruit. Nothing but desert winds and heat waves. Even worse was the lot of those who dwelled in the village of Anathoth, some four miles outside Jerusalem. Its inhabitants were priests of a special kind, notorious for the curse that lay upon them for some four hundred years: they were not allowed to officiate in the Temple. Without knowing why, they were forbidden to discharge their hereditary duties. Various stories circulated about the origins of the malediction. Some dated it back to Saul, others to Solomon. The consensus was that there must have been a family quarrel, jealousy, a dispute between their ancestors and the official priestly establishment, which had led to the exclusion of the priests at Anathoth. Was it justified? Even if it was then, surely it no longer was. Hereditary sin and/or punishment is incompatible with traditional Jewish ethics. There was no reason for Jeremiah's parents to endure discrimination for something that occurred centuries before they were born. Thus Jeremiah was a victim of injustice by virtue of his origin—he was born to one of the priests of Ana-thoth—and nothing else.

Eventually he grew and became more celebrated than most of the celebrated priests of his time—and all times—but he remained a victim. In fact, he became everybody's favorite victim: God's, Israel's, Babylon's—and Egypt's as well. There was no joy in his life, ever. No pleasant surprises, no warmth, no smiles: nothing but sorrow, anguish, and tears. Words of woe and anger—words he was made to speak against his will. He wanted to speak of other things; he wanted to be a normal person, dealing with customary human problems and not with eternity and death, but he had no choice. This is clear from the introduction to the book itself. The future prophet started out by refusing to become prophet—which is not unusual: all his predecessors since Moses had behaved that way. Prophecy is hardly a rewarding profession, being time-consuming, perilous, and, above all, lonely. One is a prophet only when the spirit of God rests on him or her. When the spirit withdraws, the prophet is left alone, alone with his memories and more vulnerable than before.

Thus Jeremiah, still young, declines God's offer and explains why; he cannot accept the position, says he, "for I cannot speak." And he continues: "I cannot speak because . . . because I am still a boy." What a peculiar pretext! What has age to do with prophecy—or God? But God's answer is also strange: "Do not invoke your youth as an excuse, for I have chosen you even before you came into this world." And He continues cryptically: "Do not worry, go where I am sending you; do not fear them, I shall stay with you." God's answer is even more obscure than Jeremiah's question. Jeremiah speaks of his youth and God gives him travel orders! Furthermore, nowhere in his argument does the prophet mention fear. Why then does God bring it up? Moreover, when God says to someone, anyone, do not fear, doesn't that mean he had better be careful?

When Jeremiah says, "I cannot speak for I am too young," he actually means: "I dare not speak; I am too young for this assignment." Then God answers: "A prophet is neither young nor old; he is ageless; he speaks in My name only when I am with him—and when I am with him, he need not fear them." Them? Whom? The others—all the others. Still, Jeremiah is reluctant. God must use force. Without waiting for the boy's decision, "the Lord put out His hand and touched my mouth, and the Lord said unto me: Herewith I put my words into your mouth." That is the end of Jeremiah's personal life, the beginning of, the initiation into, his prophetic mission. He is bound to accept and submit; there is no hiding, no running away, no seeking refuge in anonymity when God chooses to make him His emissary. From now on, Jeremiah's words will no longer be his own; whatever he says will echo God's voice.

And yet, Jeremiah really was just a boy. Though lacking experience, knowledge, and maturity, he was called upon to teach, to scold, to command and govern those who command and govern. A truly unbearable task! All children dream of being big and strong, but he dreamt of remaining a child. But God's wish is law; a prophet can and may do anything except refuse. Jeremiah becomes a prophet even before he knows it: whether he wants it or not, his life will be tied inextricably to that of his people. He lives to regret it.

In the Midrash, he tells God explicitly: "I do not want to serve You as Your prophet. I am scared. They have tried to kill all Your prophets—they will try to kill me." Later, when already a prophet, he tries to resign; he does not want to be the bearer of terrible tidings to his own people. To reassure him, God says: "You will be a prophet of doom to other nations, not to Israel." And when he does have to address himself to Israel, he turns to God and exclaims: "Why did You deceive me?" God answers: "Too late to turn the clock back; once you acquire prophetic powers, you cannot divest yourself of them." Poor Jeremiah: opposed by the mighty, hated by the masses, and even deceived by God.

Of his reluctance to assume the prophetic mantle, he says in the Midrash: "I am like the priest whose duty it is to deal with an adulteress who, he suddenly realizes, is his mother." One source maintains that, as a child, he said such things about his own mother to her face, but, seeing her distress, he corrected himself, saying: "I didn't mean you, mother; I meant mother Zion."

He is obsessed by Zion. In a poignant Midrash, the prophet says: "One day I ascended into Jerusalem and saw a woman on the top of the mountain. She was dressed in black, in mourning; her uncombed hair made her look distraught; I heard her shouting: 'Who will console me?' And I heard myself lamenting: 'Who will console me?' I spoke to her and said: 'If you are a woman, talk to me; if you are a ghost, leave me.' She answered: 'I am your mother, your mother Zion.' "

In Scripture, his real mother is not mentioned at all, and except for the name Hilkiah, nothing is said about his father. His entire childhood and adolescence are barely referred to. This is not unusual for biblical portraits, but rare for their midrashic treatment. What was he like as son, as pupil, as brother? What did he do when he had nothing to do? Where did he go when he had nowhere to go? All we know is what he tells us about others. His sermons, his predictions, his warnings: on stage, he captures our total attention; off stage, he is elusive at best. He seems to exist to illuminate other people's existences rather than to live his own.

What do we know about him? Born in the year 645 B.C.E., he began to involve himself in public affairs at the age of twenty-two; he spent more than a decade in prison; he made enemies and had few, but loyal, friends; he communicated his ideas orally and in writing; he was forbidden by God to marry and have children; he died at the age of sixty, in exile in Egypt.

From his preaching and teaching we get an astonishingly clear image of the political, religious, and social conditions in contemporary Judah. We are given a behind-the-scenes look at the politicians, the profiteers, the weak, the pacifists as well as the champions of hot or cold war, the pro-Egyptians and the pro-Babylonians—we hear their arguments and the outcome. We also get a close view of the customs and rituals of his fellow citizens: what made them run and where. Rare are the prophets who, in their moral statements, include such an avalanche of documentary material about their time.

Jeremiah's descriptive talent is both concrete and poetic. Sensitive to detail, he never stops at the surface. He captures the colors of the sky at twilight, the changing light of the desert, the thirst of the earth, the savagery of man as well as the desire of God to bring His creation closer to Him. Jeremiah always finds the proper term, the precise word to describe a landscape which, to this day, one may discover when visiting Anathoth or the hills overlooking Jerusalem at dawn. He is masterful when he communicates the mood of people awaiting war while yearning for peace; he achieves a certain tone where realistic metaphors mix with breathtaking lyricism to illustrate human frailties and moral decadence.

> Even the stork in the sky knows her seasons,
> and the turtledove, swift and crane
> keep the time of their coming;
> But my people pay no heed
> to the Law of the Lord.

The punishment?

> I will give their wives to others

and their fields to strangers. . . .
Priest and prophet alike,
they all act falsely.

And listen "to the outcry of my poor people from the land far and wide":

Harvest is past,
summer is gone,
but we have not been saved. . . .
Is there no balm in Gilead?
Can no healer be found?
Oh, that my head were water, my eyes a
fountain of tears, then I would weep
day and night for the slain of my poor
people. . . .

Even before tragedy strikes, Jeremiah's eyes behold both its victims and its perpetrators: he observes the principal characters who influence events and those who let themselves be carried by them. Kings and princes, priests and prophets, warriors and singers: he brings them to life before our eyes. The misfortunes of Jehoiachin, the hesitations of Zedekiah, the boasting of Hananiah, the collective anxiety of crowds: he sets us down in the midst of unfolding dramas. As for Jeremiah himself, we endure his helpless, angry outbursts, his violent moods, as we follow him in his walks from and to Jerusalem, as we follow his gaze into the white sand beyond the mountains of Moab and the deserts of Judah. Within the old city walls, he walks from street to street, attracting crowds that await him.

Says the Talmud: "In those times there were three prophets bringing God's word to the people. Zfanya visited the Houses of Study, Hulda sought out the women, and Jeremiah frequented the market-places." And yet, though surrounded by people, Jeremiah is alone—alone with God, and at times alone against God. Wherever he goes, he breathes misfortune, he shatters serenity. Like all prophets before him, he is constantly in the opposition, forever fighting the establishment, ridiculing power and those who hold it, emphasizing the fragility of the present, the uncertainty of the future. Listen to him and you will lose all desire to eat, drink, raise children ... Jerusalem is still vibrating with life, but he moves among its ruins; for him the city is already transported, deported faraway.

A man haunted by such visions is never popular. People avoid him, turn away from him. He is a joy-killer: he forces us to look at what we refuse to see.

No wonder that some midrashic commentators claim Jeremiah was persecuted not only by the rulers and princes of Judah but also by its general population. One feared his words, therefore one rejected the person. They called him false prophet, madman. They pushed him aside, tormented him in public, threw him into the dungeon: in short, they did everything possible to discredit him. There were those who claimed he was a descendant of Rahab, the woman of Jericho made notorious by Joshua's spies. Others went further, saying that he himself lived with a woman who resembled Rahab in her profession.

Several sources indicate that, even after the destruction, when his prophecy had been proven true, his people resented him. Those men and women in exile objected to his decision to leave them and return to Judah; the others, those who stayed behind only to be marched off to Egypt, forced him to join them. He never returned, dying somewhere in Egypt. How? He was stoned, says one midrashic source. True or not, the fact that these stories persisted shows clearly the extraordinary animosity towards him.

After all, Jeremiah represented God, the one who punished them. How could they accept him as a companion, a brother? Granted, Jeremiah tried to convince them that God too is suffering—that He too is in exile; but that brought them no comfort, it only added to their hardship.

There was something else: he reminded them of their own responsibility for their fate. He had warned them and they had refused to listen. Whenever they looked at him, they could not but remember their own shortcomings and blindness. They had to blame someone; since it could not be the enemy and surely not God, they blamed Jeremiah: he incarnated their guilty conscience, their burnt-out memory. Just as, in Judah, he had tried to make them think of the future, now, in Babylon, in defeat, he made them remember the past. If only they had listened to him . . .

But they did not listen. They were deaf to his warnings. Unwilling to hear, they were running toward catastrophe. If only they had listened to Jeremiah . . . Could the national tragedy have been averted, and the destruction of Jerusalem prevented? Aren't all historic events inevitable? Yes and no. A paradox? Not to the prophet. In his mind, the events that are yet to occur have already taken place; consequently, they still remain in the realm of fantasy.

To set Jeremiah's tale in perspective, look at his world; the planet seems glorious. Jeremiah's contemporaries or counterparts are Lao-tze, Zoroaster, Pythagoras, Siddhartha.

In Greece, Apollo and Bacchus are the stars— or the gods—of the day. In India, they go rather for the Brahmanic principles of transmigration of the soul. On Lesbos, a young poetess named Sappho indulges in certain practices which made her island famous.

The Mayas, the Etruscans, Egyptian art and Indian wisdom, Jewish prophets and Greek poetry: in the sixth century B.C.E. we witness an upsurge of culture that raises civilization to its apogee.

But it is fragmented, isolated. The great minds do not meet; the powerful voices do not mingle. Peoples do not communicate.

And what about the Jewish people?

The enmity between Judah and Israel, the two brotherly kingdoms, has left a mark on their inhabitants: as they oppose one another they oppose their common Creator. Internally weakened, Judah's political leadership is compelled to lean on one of the two superpowers: Egypt or Babylon. Its independence has been restricted to domestic affairs. Foreign policy

111

is out of its control. From time to time there develops an upsurge of religious nationalism—and then kings and princes are seized and transported deep into the land of the occupying power. For having concluded an alliance with Egypt, King Jehoiachin is exiled to Babylon. The political scientists of the time are forever weighing positions: What is better for the Jews, peace with Egypt alone, or instability on all fronts? Is neutrality really an option?

And what about God in all this? When kings cling to powerful protectors, it is always at the expense of their attachment to God. True, the Temple exists and is open for services, but read Jeremiah or Isaiah and the holy sanctuary seems something of a club. People go there to meet one another and discuss politics—or to acquire a good conscience at a reasonable price. Prayers are too bothersome. A few well-chosen offerings and all problems are solved. Who cares what one does, and with whom, since it is possible to erase everything and start all over again? The image Jeremiah likes to use is that of a prostitute. He is not against her taking money for her services, he is not even against prostitutes; he is against rulers acting as prostitutes, repeating the same words to different people, thus leaving them devoid of any meaning, forgetting the words of God —and, worse: forgetting that they have forgotten.

It is up to the prophet to stop the process by forcing them to remember: the covenant, the Law, the promise of the beginning, the moral thrust of Israel's adventure. To forget means to deny the relevance of the past. To forget the beginning means to justify the end—the end of Israel. Thus Jeremiah's magnificently rendered prophetic discourse is contrapuntal in structure and concept: set in the present, it reaches out simultaneously to the distant past and the unattainable future and makes one dependent on the other. But, while Jeremiah performs brilliantly, the audience is not with him.

So deteriorated is the moral situation, so advanced the decadence of the country that Jeremiah decides that words are no longer enough. Language is no longer a vehicle of communication.

He chooses—or God makes him choose—gestures, images, mimicry, pantomime. He breaks a bottle to demonstrate how God would break those who disobey His will. He walks in the streets of Jerusalem with a wooden yoke around his neck to warn the people that soon they too will be under the enemy's yoke. And when a false prophet breaks his wooden yoke, he puts on a new one made of iron. Do they listen, do they understand? No. They want to be defeated, they want the enemy to enter Jerusalem. ... His words frighten no one—the populace is not even moved.

And yet his vision is striking, as is his prose. Very early on, in the first period, when his sense of the impending danger is still unclear, he feels its burning shadows and speaks of a nameless enemy coming from the North. It is only after Babylon's victory over Egypt that all becomes clear in his mind and in his language: the enemy is Babylon—for Babylon is strong and invincible, which Judah is not, since it is no longer protected by God. And why has God withdrawn His protection from Judah? Because Judah did not seek it, though it needed protection more than ever. Babylon is invincible because God wants it to be invincible. "My servant Nebuchadnezzar," says God through the voice of Jeremiah. The enemy Nebuchadnezzar, the invader, the destroyer of Jerusalem, is God's servant? Is this conceivable? If so, how can one resist anger or madness? Once he understands the situation, Jeremiah is tempted by despair, he is seduced by the idea of total and ultimate resignation. Scripture does not say so, but it would not be out of character for him to give up his impossible, inhuman mission. Since he is not free to do that, he allows his anger to explode: first against the people who refuse to grasp the seriousness of the situation, then against God Himself, who is using him as a powerless tool, and finally, against the victorious enemy. In the end everyone is vanquished; Babylon too will be destroyed—and God Himself is in mourning. In the cosmic catastrophe that Jerusalem's destruction represents, there is no winner.

The prophet knows it; he alone knows it. Therein lies his insoluble dilemma: if tragedy strikes, is it not because of his foreknowledge of that tragedy? What is he supposed to do with his knowledge? If he reveals it, the dreaded event may not come to pass. In other words: only if he tells the truth about what may and will happen is there a chance for it not to happen; only if he tells the truth can it prove to be false!

Jeremiah fascinates and stirs us endlessly, and

disturbs as well. Too unstable? Yes. Too dramatic? Yes. Too clairvoyant? Yes again. A man who knows so much—who has access to such high sources—is not easy to live with.

Also: he is too serious, too solemn; he never laughs, never cheers, never utters a sentence which is not appropriate and heaven-inspired. How can anyone cope with a man who only repeats what God tells him?

When all is said and done, we still fail to understand how he can be so severe, so harsh towards his people. If anyone were to repeat today what he said about Israel, we would immediately call him an anti-Semite. God orders him to assume the role of prosecutor, probably because He finds him suitable for it. Jeremiah should protest more frequently and with more vigor, and more conviction. He could say, as other spokesmen have done before and after him: "Look at other nations too, O Lord; are they better than Israel?"

His pacifism has some immediate implications as well; it could not help but weaken the morale of the Jewish nation and its leaders. What he demands is surrender to the enemy, without a fight, without any attempt to resist. He advocates total, unconditional surrender, abdication of all that bears the mark of Jewish sovereignty, capitulation of all the fighting forces. Humiliation on a national scale—that is what the prophet suggests and indeed demands. Even if one understands his courageous speeches before the war, one must resent them during the war. They surely contributed to the defeat.

A disturbing episode: he confronts a false prophet—a certain Hananiah—who, optimistic and exuberant, predicts that the Babylonian exile will last only two years, after which the king, the warriors, and their families will return to Zion. The nightmare will be lifted and Jews will smile again, laugh again, rejoice again. Responds Jeremiah—the man of unbending principles, the bearer of truth: "Amen—may your predictions come true." And he goes away. That was wrong, as many scholars agree. Jeremiah was duty-bound to speak up. Either he is sure of himself and of God, or he is not. If not, he has no right to demoralize an entire nation; if he is sure, he is obliged to confront Hananiah and tell him the truth: that his illusions are dangerous, as illusions always are. His "Amen" is out of place. From Jeremiah we expect words of truth, not clichés of compromise. The spokesman for God thus becomes an echo for a false prophet. Between God and Hananiah, he chooses Hananiah?

Another troubling episode: in the middle of the catastrophe, Jeremiah involves himself in some startling activities. The capital is besieged and the prophet is in jail. Nebuchadnezzar has been ruler for eighteen years and his empire has expanded into and beyond the kingdom of Judah, which is near collapse. Suddenly Jeremiah receives the visit of his uncle Hanamel, son of Shallum, who begins to talk to him about real estate. The uncle offers to sell him his property. Almost a whole chapter is devoted to this business deal: the price, the conditions, the motives. The world is trembling, heaven and earth are in turmoil, and all Jeremiah is concerned with is a piece of property he is purchasing from his uncle!

And one final disappointment: Jeremiah should go to Babylon and stay there; he should choose exile and suffer with those who, under hostile skies, along the shores of foreign rivers filled with Jewish blood, are marching with heavy hearts and bowed heads toward the unkown. He may have good reasons to be separated from the people in peace, but not in war; in victory, not in suffering; in Judah, not in Babylon.

In his description of King Zedekiah's end, the old king is taken prisoner by the enemy and forced to witness the massacre of his children. Then—and only then—is he made blind.

Why doesn't the prophet join his king? Why does he stay behind? This question is even more painful in the Midrash, where Jeremiah is described leaving the exiled in Babylon and returning to Judah: the text shows the exiled pleading with the prophet, urging him not to abandon them but to share their grief, their longing, their pain. But their pleas fall on deaf ears. He prefers to return to the ruins of Judah, the familiar grounds of what used to be a Jewish city, a Jewish street, a Jewish home. Is this behavior worthy of a prophet in Israel?

What does one do when confronted by a difficult and obscure text? One reads it again and again, and discovers another layer beneath the visible, another dimension, another meaning; and ultimately, one makes peace with its hidden significance.

First, let us examine the other characters: they

all seem second-rate. The kings are either weak or wicked or both. Their subjects are complacent. They all crave power and fortune, they all seek luxury, comfort, and promiscuity. They admire the soothing, reassuring false prophets who demand no sacrifice and no effort, who offer easy answers to difficult questions and appeal to popular taste at its lowest. When Jeremiah dares to be nonconformist, they beat him up, send him to jail. He is saved not by a prince but by a foreign servant, a black man.

God Himself does not come off too well: not only is He hard to understand and impossible to follow, but He is constantly complaining, forever angry, threatening, thundering. Why is He upset—and why only with the Jews? Nebuchadnezzar kills and destroys—yet he fares better than his victims. To make things worse, he is shown as a reluctant invader, an unwilling conqueror: God has to force him to win his wars against the Jews. Why is God acting like that? To make Israel repent? Why not perform a miracle instead? Why does He have to use violence and death as leverage? He wants to prove that He is almighty. Obstinate, unyielding, merciless, He does what He wants. But what about pity, grace, compassion for innocent children? He weeps later? We can do without His tears.

So we see there is no hero in this story. In a way, Jeremiah is an anti-hero, eliciting conflicting reactions from us. Some of his shortcomings seem like virtues. We even begin to like him for his weaknesses. If, at first, we resented his excessive suffering, now we try to alleviate it. He does not enjoy it after all; he never did. He never sought pain; quite the contrary: he only tried to disarm it. Since he could not avoid it, he tried to redeem it, to transform it from within.

An example: to the exiled King Jehoiachin in Babylon, he writes a letter which can serve as a blueprint for Jewish life in the Diaspora: "Build homes and dwell in them. Plant orchards and eat their fruit. Gives wives to your sons, husbands to your daughters —let them have children. Multiply wherever you are, do not decrease in numbers. And seek peace for the land in which you live, for if there is peace there, there will be peace everywhere."

He advocates a synthesis, a symbiosis, between the land of Israel and the people of Israel. "Since you are in the Diaspora," he tells his exiled king, "do something to give it meaning. Otherwise you will come closer to despair—and despair has no place in Jewish history."

Why does he insist again and again on Nebuchadnezzar's being God's emissary? By placing the Babylonian king under God's authority, Jeremiah seems to be undermining Israel's faith in its own future, its own ability to fight for a future. But that is wrong. If Jeremiah invokes God's name, it is because he knows that Israel's suffering is inevitable— and he wants to lend it meaning. Nothing is worse than suffering ... except meaningless suffering. And the meaning has to be found in the suffering itself.

Another example of Jeremiah's sensitivity and greatness: take the puzzling episode of Hananiah and his false prophecy. Jeremiah seems to acquiesce too quickly, to approve Hananiah's optimism. That too is wrong. It may well be his way of expressing defiance —of stifling a voice not his own, of turning it away from a vision imposed on him. Even earlier, he said so many terrible things and predicted so many catastrophes to so many families—he probably prefers not to believe in them himself; he probably wishes to discard them as silly fears and premonitions. Perhaps he would like to tell his people: "Listen to me, do you think for one moment that I enjoy my role? That I derive pleasure from predicting a future of ashes for you? Hananiah is optimistic and God is not—well, amen, may Hananiah be right!" Quite possibly, by approving Hananiah, Jeremiah hopes to transform his falsehood into truth; in other words, he hopes to force God's hand. After all, God will not deny both His true and false prophets. Facing Hananiah and his cheerful mood, Jeremiah discovers that he too would like to be cheerful, a man like all others, who aspires to hope with and for the others, a man who yearns to justify faith in creation, in life. Yes, Jeremiah yields to weakness: he is human, after all.

Human in dealing both with theological concepts and small things. As André Neher points out in his definitive book on Jeremiah, the prophet's decision to turn away from collective tragedy long enough to purchase a plot of land is far from petty or senseless; it has purpose.

That purpose is to teach his contemporaries and

their descendants a lesson: there comes a time when one must look away from death and turn away from the dead; one must cling to life, which is made of minutes, not necessarily years, and surely not centuries; one must fight so as not to be overwhelmed by history but to act upon it concretely, simply, humanly. In the midst of national catastrophe, one must continue to teach and study, bake and sell bread, plant trees and count on the future. One must not wait for the tragedy to end before building or rebuilding life; one must do it in the very face of tragedy. The city is besieged? People are hungry? Children are afraid? And the prophet is in jail? No matter: he meets with his uncle, negotiates contracts, pays money, and proclaims: *Od yibanu batim—*"do not worry, my brothers. Many more houses will be rebuilt in this land of destruction."

For this urgent and profoundly stirring lesson alone, we cherish Jeremiah. More than most prophets, he offers us an example of behavior, not before or after, but during periods of pressure, stress, and peril.

Though alone, he defines himself in relation to his fellowmen, who reject him. Though shattered, he does not try to escape the present and seek refuge in the future; he works with the present, on the present. Living in a disorganized, dehumanized world, he forces himself to pick up the broken pieces and dreams of man's possibilities to create harmony.

Jeremiah abides by God's law but disputes His justice. He declines the responsibility of moral leadership in the beginning; he does not wish to serve God as prophet. He says, "I want to remain a child." He becomes a prophet only when he thinks he can prevent disaster; once he realizes he cannot, he protests forcefully. "Of course, God, You are just and righteous; but I shall quarrel with You, I have no choice: it is because You are just and Your name is truth that I must quarrel with You. Ah, if only I could go and hide in the desert, and stay away from society." Only from society? No, from God as well. Like Jonah, he yearns to run, to go underground, to escape a destiny outlined by God. Few prophets have spoken up with such anguish and forcefulness against heavenly injustice—or heavenly justice, which is worse.

We criticized him for not staying with the exiled in Babylon. Well, he does try. The Midrash describes him seeking out children, embracing and kissing them. When he finds a group of tormented young men, he joins them and wants to share their pain. When a number of Jews are about to be hanged, he tries to hang himself: he wants to die with them but does not succeed. The enemy won't allow it. General Nebuzaradan tells him: "I have orders to keep you alive." Jeremiah must stay alive because the enemy does not want him to die. Even when he suffers, he remains alone, separated from his people. And so he finally decides not to stay with them in Babylon. He knows he is not like them and never will be: that he is condemned to suffer apart, to die apart. The knowledge that so many of them will perish while he remains an onlooker is unbearable to him. And so he returns to Judah—with his memories.

Then and there, the circle is closed. The prophet of Israel has become the prophet to all nations. He now understands—and makes others understand—that Israel's destiny affects everyone else's. What happens to Judah will eventually happen to Babylon, then Rome, and ultimately, to the entire world. And so the most Jewish of the Jewish prophets becomes the most universal among them.

Jeremiah appeals to us as a writer, a modern chronicler, above all; his obsessions are ours. And so are his themes. Listen to some examples:

Doubt and self-doubt: Will he be able to tell a tale that defies language and reason? Will he be worthy of his mission? Will he succeed in communicating the message? Will people believe him? He reminds us of the ghetto-survivor who returned from Ponar and Treblinka to warn his friends, but who was unable to make them pay attention.

Solitude: No solitude is greater than that of the messenger who is unable to transmit the message. No one is as alone as the prophet whom God chooses to isolate from those he is sent to warn and save. No one is as alone as the man who must speak and is not heard.

Despair: Jeremiah's mood often borders on hopelessness. Listen:

> My heart is broken within me . . . .
> I am like a drunken man . . . .
> I have become a laughingstock
> all these days; everyone mocks me;
> for as often as I speak I have to cry out,
> and complain of violence and abuse . . . .

He remains a bachelor. Is it only because of God's injunction: "You will not want to marry and have children"? More likely, as Jeremiah has little if any faith in mankind, he surely can see no justification for bringing children into a world doomed by its own forces.

Protest: against man and his blindness, against God and His silence. Waiting: At the end of the story we read that the prophet asks God the very question he had been asked by leaders of Judah: What were they to do? And God waits ten days before He answers. Try to imagine those ten days and you may feel what Jews felt in their ghettos somewhere in Eastern Europe and elsewhere as well.

Testimony: Jeremiah does not stop talking, dictating, writing down every dream, every command, every whisper, every anecdote, every episode, every moan and outcry. He knows his voice will not carry, and yet: he yells, shouts, warns, pleads, prays. He has no choice: he must do something with his life. If he survives, it must be for a reason; he must do something with every minute—for every minute is a minute of grace.

And the last theme: consolation. Jeremiah stops chastising and begins comforting his people. Therein too lies his singularity: the same prophet who witnessed suffering describes the end of suffering; the chronicler of destruction sings the beginning of consolation.

Jeremiah is therefore the first—and most eloquent—among Jewish writers of all times. We still use his vocabulary to describe our experiences. In fact, he is the most quoted among the prophets; his words apply to all circumstances. *Shalom, Shalom vein Shalom,* "everyone speaks of peace and there is no peace." *Shfokh hamatcha al hagoyim,* "punish those who reject you." The expression *Katzon latevach,* "like sheep to slaughter," has become almost a cliché. *Palit vesarid,* "the refugee, the survivor," is also his. Or: *Lo alman Israel,* "Israel is still not widowed, abandoned." Some passages in the book are reflected in the Holocaust chronicles of Ringelblum, Dweorzecki, and Kaplan.

Like them, he never knew whether his writings would see the light of day, whether future generations would know the truth.

Some modern words or expressions gain a new meaning only when used within a biblical context—and the other way around. Some biblical metaphors become clear only when used within our own experience.

Listen to Jeremiah:

"I look at the skies and their light is gone. I look at the mountains and they are quaking. I look: no man is left, and all the birds of the sky have fled . . . ."

Quaking mountains? What did Jeremiah mean to convey? I never understood the meaning of these words until I visited Babi-Yar. Eyewitnesses had told me that, in September 1941, when the German invaders massacred some 80,000 Jews—between Rosh Hashana and Yom Kippur—and buried them in the ravine, near the center of Kiev, the ground was shaking for weeks on end. The mountains of corpses made the earth quake . . And I understood Jeremiah.

As for the birds of the sky that have fled, I understood the prophet's imagery only when I returned to Auschwitz and Birkenau in the summer of 1979. Then and only then did I remember that, during the tempest of fire and silence, there were no birds to be seen on the horizon: they had fled the skies above all the death-camps. I stood in Birkenau and remembered Jeremiah.

One day the prophet's faithful friend and scribe Baruch ben Neriah was arrested and brought before the king, who wanted to read Jeremiah's book. The scene took place in the royal winter palace. The king stood before the fireplace and read Jeremiah's tales and then destroyed them. Calmly, systematically, he would read one scroll and throw it into the flames, take the next one and the next—until finally Jeremiah's masterwork was reduced to ashes. Any other writer would have lost his mind. Not Jeremiah. He simply began writing the book all over again—adding the story of the destruction of the first version. And therein lies Jeremiah's ultimate lesson for all tellers of tales: to rewrite is more difficult and more important than to write; to transmit is more vital than to invent.

And what are we doing, we writers, we witnesses, we Jews? For over three thousand years we have been repeating the same story—the story of a solitary prophet who would have given anything, including his life, to be able to tell another kind of tale, one filled with joy and fervor rather than sorrow and anguish.

But he transmitted only what he received—and so do we. And if God was angry at him for not weeping, we are not. Quite the contrary: we are proud of him. The world was not worthy of his tears. Or ours.

Jonah

A strange character, he resembles no one in Scripture. No one has had his problems, or suggestions regarding their solution.

Is he a prophet? If so, why is there no official reference to such a title? A man who argues with God not to save men but to punish them—what kind of prophet is that anyway?

Jonah is clumsy, less than lucky. He does not feel wanted or at home anywhere. He shows up where least expected. And refuses to go where he is supposed to go.

What does he want? Why is it that he, of all people, opposes both the Almighty and His weak, vulnerable human creatures? If, at least, he were someone influential or great: a prince like Isaiah, a royal adviser like Nathan, a witness like Jeremiah . . . But, though we know little about him, we do know that he was not celebrated, nor did he participate in any of the great dramatic upheavels in the history of the Jewish people.

Jonah is "a minor prophet," the poor man's

prophet. To be precise, he is the fifth in a series of twelve, whose words we remember, but not their lives. In Jonah's case however, it is just the opposite.

His story is presented on prime-time, on Yom Kippur, but not until *Mincha* services, at dusk, when everyone is tired, hungry, and waiting for the climactic chanting of *Neila*. One might almost consider Jonah's story as incidental, an afterthought, a so-called filler.

Poor prophet, he entertains rather than disturbs, he makes his readers smile rather than weep.

And yet, on reading his story, we realize that he also moves us to think more deeply. And to dream more fervently.

At the mention of his name one's mind begins to wander in search of adventure and enchantment; we think of the whale, hear the roaring tempest, roam the streets of noisy cities with their seductive nightlife and their corrupting daylife; we watch the sky and expect it to burst open at any moment and send down fire and brimstone upon all those who forget that the earth too is the Lord's. Thus, the Book of Jonah may be read as the novel of Jonah—a work of pure fiction with religious and theological overtones, and with even a page or so for the ecologists as well. As such, the story is appealing in its simplicity and naiveté, and, above all, its drama.

It is a story about waiting—waiting for events to unfold, about things that are expected to happen but do not. We are kept breathlessly on the edge, miraculously prevented from taking the last step. Jonah runs away, but not far enough. The boat is in danger of sinking, but stays afloat. Jonah almost dies, Nineveh is almost destroyed. One might describe it as a unique suspense story—for children—with a magnificent happy ending. Vanished, the fears. Gone, the ominous predictions. All personal and national catastrophes are averted. Everybody involved is pleased: Nineveh, because it avoids punishment; God, because He succeeds, without really trying, in saving Nineveh from punishment. The reader too is happy: if the wicked people of Nineveh escape with impunity and continue to live and flourish, why not everyone else?

As for Jonah, is he, too, pleased with the outcome? What has he gained in the test that pits him against all the other characters in the cast?

The story begins as God orders a certain Jonah, son of Amittai, to hurry to Nineveh and warn its inhabitants to repent lest their city be destroyed in forty days. Prophet of both doom and consolation, he ought to accept the divine assignment: after all, that is his profession, his calling. As God's emissary, he must obey His will if he hopes to move others to do likewise. It is probably not his first mission, but it is his first refusal: he does not wish to go to Nineveh. In other words, he does precisely what he has been ordered to tell Nineveh not to do: he resists God's will. So determined is he that he decides to run away. He buys a ticket and boards a ship going from Jaffa to Tarshish, the opposite direction from Nineveh. Why Tarshish? Are its people more righteous than those of Nineveh? We do not know, nor are we supposed to care. What matters is that Jonah goes farther and farther away from Nineveh, and from God.

Second act: caught in a sudden storm, the boat is about to sink. The crew gives up hope and resorts to prayer. In vain. One sailor remembers a passenger who has not been seen praying: Jonah. He is found below, sound asleep in his cabin. The crew wakes him up, orders him to come up on deck. Surely one among the passengers is responsible for the impending disaster. They draw lots and soon turn on Jonah: he is the culprit. He readily confesses and even suggests his punishment: to be thrown into the sea. He wishes to die, and the crew obliges by throwing him overboard.

Third act: the scene shifts from the ship to an immense whale sent by God to swallow and save Jonah, who stays inside the whale three days and three nights; he is uncomfortable, he implores God's mercy; he repents; he will go to Nineveh, he will preach, he will do anything, say anything, anywhere —but please, God, free him from his underwater prison!

Fourth act: out of the whale, out of the water, Jonah hurries to Nineveh, speaks in the name of God, and, wonder of wonders, the people listen and repent. This pleases God, but displeases His emissary, who is more disturbed by his success than by his failure. Again, he wishes to die. On the outskirts of the city, he builds himself a hut as protection from the blazing sun. Interestingly, a plant—a Kikayon—grows above his head, conveniently offering him some shade. At last, Jonah is happy. But not for long. At dawn, the poor plant is devoured by a worm. Gone, the protecting shadow. The unrelenting heat causes Jonah to faint. Again, he wants to die: no prophet has ever been gripped by so strong and so recurrent a death wish. What a perfect opportunity for God to teach him a lesson: Jonah, Jonah, you felt pity for a plant but not for a human community? Really, Jonah . . .

There is no fifth act, at least not in the script. The dialogue comes to an abrupt end. God wins the argument since Jonah is unable to refute it. But what happens then? If there is an answer, nobody knows it. No sooner has the question been touched upon, inferentially, than the story is finished. Poor prophet: he is not even informed of the dénouement of his own story.

Upon close scrutiny, we cannot fail to find something altogether disturbing, even upsetting, about the story: it is too superficial, its plot too transparent; all these miracles, all these surprises are too predictable. The book lacks inspiration, logic, and, above all, prophecy.

If Jonah wishes that much to die, why does he cling to life? Why does he seek the coolness of the shade, when he should do nothing to avoid suffering? His is a peculiar combination of life-force and death wish. Which is more real?

Why is he so determined to allow destiny to crush Nineveh? Why is he bent on sabotaging its repentance and chance of survival? What kind of prophet would prevent a people from returning to God's ways? By acting as he does, hasn't the prophet suddenly turned anti-prophet?

But then, was he ever a prophet? He is described as such by the reader, not the author. In the book bearing his name all we find is an extravaganza about a man who, why not say it, appears to be more of a misfit than a hero. His prophecy consists of only one sentence: "In forty days Nineveh will be destroyed." The rest centers around a whale and a plant.

The man is also disturbing because of the secrecy surrounding his biographical data. What we do know about him is that he was strange—in fact, so strange that, in some circles, he was looked upon not as one person but two.

In other words: there lived a man named Jonah, son of Amittai, and there was a Book of Jonah, but while that man was the prophet, he was not the author of the book.

According to this theory, the first Jonah lived in the eighth century B.C.E., and the book was written some five centuries later. The book contains certain technical terms invented not under King Jeroboam but much later. To solve the mystery of the five-hundred-year delay, some experts have chosen to deal with two men named Jonah: any detective will affirm that it is easier to deal with a double mystery than with a single one. Any novelist will confirm that it is easier to enlarge the action and the cast than to create one single, complex character.

With two Jonahs on our hands, we may have

solved the problems of language, but not those of history and philosophy. We know pitifully little about the first Jonah, son of Amittai. And even less about the second.

Of the first, we are told in the Second Book of Kings he was dispatched by God to convince the wicked King Jeroboam to mend his ways, and he failed. Of the second, we learn he was sent to Nineveh on a similar mission but one that was crowned with success.

Of course, it is the latter that interests us. First, because of the story itself. Second, because of Jonah's obvious taste for failure and tragedy. And third, because of his profession; after all, he was a writer—and a good one at that.

Fantasy, imagination, vocabulary: Jonah's book is so well written that one is not suprised by his lack of success. Unhappy, unlucky always. Rarely does anything good happen to him. No honors, no rewards, no friends, no supporters. Whatever he undertakes seems to go wrong. Whenever he wishes to win, he loses; whenever he would prefer to lose, he wins. He is a displaced person, living in an internal exile. The quintessential anti-hero, he takes no initiative, aspires to no glory, works on no grandiose scheme to change life or history. Completely passive, he lets others worry and make decisions for him. Instead of shaping events, he lets himself be carried by them. Instead of guiding people, he allows them to push him around. He appears on stage only to question God, or himself. "What am I doing here? Why have I been sent here? What is the meaning of these things

I have been involved in?" He is always looking for answers, always seeking some kind of assurance that he has not boarded the wrong ship.

Actually, even his questions are wrong. Rather than ask why God should send him on a futile mission to Nineveh, he ought to ask: "Why must I go? True, I am your prophet, but a prophet is human, hence free. I may choose not to go to Nineveh: isn't it man's goal to deepen his own sense of freedom?"

Instead, he acknowledges his duty to obey the travel orders and his inability to follow through. And then, he runs away, like a child afraid of being scolded. Of all people, Jonah, a divine messenger, should know that geography has nothing to do with theology, and that starting with Adam, man has never been able to hide from God; God is always swifter than man and arrives first everywhere, even when He leaves last. Man can run away from man, but not from God. Why then did the prophet, chosen by the Almighty to serve as His preacher, His emissary, suddenly decide to behave like a runaway slave?

Elijah fled from Jezebel, Jeremiah from Jehoiakim, but only Jonah fled fom God. Didn't he know he had to lose? Once he took the wrong turn, all that followed was inevitably doomed to failure. At every step, he realizes he has made another mistake. He boards a ship only to fall into the ocean. He falls into the ocean only to save the ship: for the ship to remain afloat, he has to jump overboard.

Except for his one initiative to escape, he passively allows things to happen. The whale swallows him, holds him, and frees him; he has nothing to do with it. Someone else pulls the strings, someone else charts the course. The text often emphasizes that fact: God is the director of the drama in which Jonah performs. Is he the star? No, not really. The wind in the story, says the Talmud, was created before Creation for the sole purpose of provoking the tempest which threatens to wreck the boat. Were it not for that wind, there would be no story. Thus the wind has a starring part. So too does the whale, who performs impressively: keeping a human being alive in its belly for three days and three nights, after all, is something to be proud of. Jonah is the object rather than the subject of a story which he dislikes and rightly so: it does not do him justice.

Jonah seems to appear only to emphasize his own vulnerability, his own frequent downfalls. Nineveh will be saved, against his will, which means: he will succeed against his will. At the end, he feels not only useless, superfluous, but also guilty: has God not given and taken back the plant, the Kikayon, only to prove a point? Jonah came to love that Kikayon. He must have loved it more than anything in the world because it offered him protection and asked nothing in return. And now it had died because of him, or rather because of God, who wanted to teach him a lesson. In a way, the plant died for him.

And so Jonah would appear to be the perfect illustration of the anti-hero in Scripture, having been a complete failure all his life and in all his endeavors: he fails as a prophet, since he chooses to become an anti-prophet; he fails as a fugitive, since he does show up in Nineveh. He even fails in his death wish:

twice he asks to die only to survive and live in remorse. Has there ever been a more frustrated prophet in the Bible?

No wonder he refuses to obey God when ordered to go to Nineveh: Jonah says, "No—no, thank you."

To be fair, we must recall other prophets who have also said "no" to God. He was neither the first nor the only one. Even Moses argued with God and said: "Why me? You need a messenger—send someone else!" And remember Jeremiah and his excuses. "I am only a child," he said. "You need a grown-up, a man of experience."

But Jonah is different: he is the first—and the only one—to reject his mission not only in words but in deed: he flees the country. In the true tradition of romantic fugitives, he sails off into the sunset.

But what if his resistance itself was willed by God? And what if his escape from Nineveh was designed to bring him back to Nineveh? Why did he not think that far ahead? Why did he contradict himself so often? Technically, a prophet whose predictions do not come true is considered a false prophet. And yet, Jonah remains a true prophet. How is one to understand his complex and bizarre destiny?

What makes our task even more difficult is the almost total lack of information about him. His file in Scripture is astonishingly meager: his name and the name of his father, nothing else. Where does he dwell? Mystery. When? No date is indicated. Who are his friends, his teachers, his enemies? Impossible to ascertain. What was he doing until the incident that made him famous? What became of him afterwards? Nobody tells us. Without Nineveh and its sinners, Jonah might not have figured in sacred Jewish history—and neither would the whale.

All we find in the text is a sober, realistic description of the only event we are ordered to remember about him. The story is like a Chekhov play: Jonah refuses to obey, Jonah obeys, Jonah has obeyed. The end.

Fortunately, the Talmud, as always, is more generous, endowing its biblical portraits with more imagination and greater detail. One source places Jonah after David and Samuel. We are even asked to believe he was equal to Elijah, who ordained him as prophet.

Midrashic legends describe him as *Tzaddik gam-our*—a true Just man, an absolute Just man, among the few chosen to enter Paradise alive.

One source finds it necessary and significant to mention that Jonah seems to have been wealthy, a conclusion based on his being able to buy a boat ticket and not having to travel as a stowaway. One text tells us something even funnier, namely that the ticket cost more than the ship itself.

The midrashic imagination covers his wife as well, a woman—unfortunately anonymous—so pious that three times a year she went on pilgrimage to Jerusalem and the Sages did not object. Faithful to custom, the midrashic storytellers pay attention to secondary characters as well. The sailors, for instance, are not just simple sailors; they represent the "United Nations," so to speak, expressing themselves in seventy tongues and praying—but in vain—to all the existing gods to rescue them. After witnessing Jonah's successful intercession with his God, they throw their idols into the sea, sail back to the Jaffa harbor, go to Jerusalem and, says the text: "return their wives to God"—whatever that may mean—"and become learned men."

The midrashic description of the tempest itself is almost three-dimensional: we see the boat as it bobs haplessly on the water, we hear it cracking, we see the crew members running around in despair, we hear their laments. They do not want to throw Jonah into the ocean, but they must. The moment he is overboard, the sea quiets down. They bring him back, and immediately the sea starts raging again. This game goes on and on, and is interrupted only by the whale, which has no taste for games. Says the Midrash: "Jonah entered the mouth of the whale as one enters a synagogue."

Still—poor Jonah: one can easily imagine how he felt as the crew made him go back and forth. A quick death would have been more merciful. The world was against him; everybody wanted him dead, except the whale.

But then, didn't Jonah want Nineveh dead?

Seen from this angle, the story of Jonah intrigues us even more than before, for it sheds a gloomy light on all its characters. All are reprehensible, all are guilty.

Let us look at Nineveh. Its guilt self-evident; it is a city filled with sin, with a population manifesting an ancestral hated towards Israel, whose antithe-

Jonah

sis it represents. In biblical imagery Nineveh is made
to symbolize war, deceit, envy, and cruelty, and therefore deserves death. It ranks not far behind Sodom.

What about the crew? Guilty as charged, they
dispose of a helpless passenger in order to save their
own skins. Never mind that it is he himself who
asks them to cast him into the sea. Since when must
one oblige a person with suicidal tendencies? One
may argue that the sailors are not really anti-Semites,
that their predicament is such that they would do
the same to anyone else—that is, manifest the same
selfishness, the same thirst for survival. They would
show no less cruelty to any other victim, regardless
of his or her race, color, or creed, which is not new.
We know from experience that whoever hates Jews
will end up hating all men; whoever hates one
group does in fact hate mankind. In any case, the
sailors are not appealing human beings. We may not
choose life at the expense of another. Jewish law
says that a community must never hand over one of
its own members to the enemy even if refusal means
death for the entire community. Although Jonah is
not one of their own, he is their guest, their passenger. Don't they know that a ship's crew is duty-bound
to save the lives of the passengers before their own?
And remember: Jonah is not a stowaway; he has,
after all, paid his fare.

Even the sea is guilty—and the wind too. Why
do they interfere? If God has problems with Jonah
and Jonah with Nineveh, why do they have to get
involved?

If God wishes to punish or test Jonah, the sea

141

has no reason to offer its services. Has the wind been created solely for that purpose? Could it not argue with God: "Listen, Almighty God, I understand that I must help You test Jonah, but he is not alone aboard that ship! There are other people on it! And they are not participants in this game, are they? I understand that You might want Jonah to become seasick, but why them? I understand that You might want Jonah to sense death approaching, but why them? You want me to help You punish or at least worry Jonah—so be it! But do not expect me to deliberately frighten innocent bystanders!"

As for the whale, it must have frightened its unexpected visitor and prisoner, however unintentionally. The Zohar says explicitly that Jonah died of fear—but came back to life. It was Jonah's most painful experience; he says so himself. His plea reverberates in our own to this very day. We still evoke that episode in our prayers: "Answer us, oh God, as You answered Jonah while he was inside the whale." A prisoner of both the ocean and the whale, his prayer is heartbreaking. Does the whale really have to obey God? Could it not ask God what evil it has committed to be forced to inflict such suffering "onto this man who is His and His alone?" True, the whale saves Jonah. But why only after three days and three nights? Why not have it spit him back ashore right away?

Each of the elements can put the blame on God: after all, just as they are responsible to Him, He is responsible for them. In fact, He is both author and director of the drama. As such, sadly, His role is not too flattering. One gets the impression that He singles out Jonah only to mock him—and that He consecrates him as prophet only so that the whole world can ridicule him. After all, He sends him to Nineveh knowing that, either way, people will laugh at him. If they don't listen to his sermons, they will laugh while he is delivering them; if they do listen, they will laugh at him afterwards. God knows what no one else knows, that Nineveh will not be destroyed, and yet He is sending Jonah to predict its destruction! At least, if Jonah were allowed to use the subjunctive mode, the conditional tense, and to say: "Beware, if you do not repent, your city may be reduced to ashes." But his warning is precise and clear, final and irrevocable: "In forty days Nineveh will be destroyed." Too late for remorse, too late for penitence. But it was not too late: everybody knows that when it comes to repentance, it is never too late. Only Jonah is led to believe otherwise. Why does God order His servant to bypass truth? Why does He choose to turn him into a buffoon, thus depriving him of his right to pride and dignity? God does everything to humiliate His prophet: He makes him lie, suffer, and eventually disappear! He goes so far as to cut him off! He prevents him from talking! The last word in the Book of Jonah is not Jonah's but God's.

And yet—some blame must also be put on Jonah. Why is he so hostile to people he doesn't even know? They may not be pious, but they are human. In the name of divine, abstract justice, he is ready to condemn them all, to see them all perish. Doesn't he know that, in the eyes of God and man, ideas and beautiful phrases are less important than human beings? His self-image stands between him and this knowledge; his concern is with that image and not with other people's lives and welfare. Is he ready to see an entire city fall into ruins only to safeguard his reputation as a prophet? Does he want Nineveh destroyed only because he has predicted it? Does he forget what Moses did—and would do—in similar circumstances? "Let me die," Moses said, "but do not touch one child in Israel!" That is what Jonah should have said: "Let me tell lies, but I don't want human beings killed! When it comes to saving a community —with its men and women, its children—I do not count!" Why does he say the opposite? The moment he senses that Nineveh is meant to live on, he becomes angry. Listen carefully to the text: it is the survival of a city rather than its destruction that angers Jonah. But then, how is one to feel sympathy for his problems? For centuries Jews have been beseeching the Almighty to be more compassionate with His children, and now Jonah wants Him to be less compassionate?

Thus Jonah seems the least attractive of all the characters in the story. Let us reread the passage of the tempest: The wind is howling, the waves are roaring, the ship is about to break up into a thousand pieces; everybody is busy, everybody tries to help, some work, others pray, all efforts, all energies are being mobilized; everybody is trying to be useful except Jonah. What is his contribution to the collective rescue operation? Incredible but true: in that hour of crisis and mortal danger, when the world is upside down, when creation is in turmoil, the prophet —who should, by definition, be more sensitive, more alert, more tense than the common mortal—is asleep! Instead of sounding the alarm and leading the rescue activities, he goes on sleeping! What kind of prophet is he? Why shouldn't people refuse to listen to his sermons? And why shouldn't God mock him?

But if every one of the participants is to be blamed, why are they all invited into the sacred Yom Kippur services? Do they too need atonement and forgiveness? What is the moral of the story?

One thing is clear: the story is more complex than it appears on the surface. The various situations hide more than they reveal. As for the characters, they live on more than one level and show more than one face.

And so, when we reread the story, we discover that it can easily be turned around: just as we said earlier that all the characters are guilty, we may now claim that all are innocent. And infinitely appealing.

Let us begin with Nineveh: granted, its inhabitants are wicked—why shouldn't they be? They live in a large urban development. And there is no one to teach them, to warn them, to show them the right way. As soon as they hear Jonah, they accept the message and repent, as the text says. The king is the first to confess his sins; he proclaims a state of national penitence. And all the inhabitants—young and old, men and women, the animals too—join in solidarity and prayer. The Talmud quotes examples to illustrate their metamorphosis: they pay their debts; they return what does not belong to them; they help and care for one another.

Life becomes bearable. Better yet: although they have forty days to change their ways to avert the catastrophe, they do not wait until the thirty-ninth to do penance but begin immediately. They repent on the very first day, not the last. Are they not worthy of praise, those so-called wicked people of Nineveh?

As for the sailors, we were too harsh on them also. They are actually polite and helpful. At the moment of danger, they do not jump into the water to save their own skins but remain together and begin to work—together—to save the ship and all its passengers. As the danger increases, they dispose of objects—their own valuables, their own precious belongings. When they discover their troublesome passenger sound asleep below deck, they could cover him with angry insults but do not. They are not even angry. The captain himself takes the trouble to wake him, gently, softly, in a friendly manner. *Ma lekha, nirdam?* he wants to know, "How come you fell asleep?" or "What happened to you, sleeper?" His voice is calm, courteous, almost poetic. He should send Jonah upstairs and put him to work but does not. With tongue-in-cheek, he asks him—and this is perhaps the third interpretation of his question— whether it is with his sleeping that he hopes to save the ship from going under. Then, becoming serious, he asks him to pray to his God. When all prayers fail, they draw lots and Jonah emerges as suspect. Clearly, this is not the crew's doing, it is destiny's.

They question him and he tells them his story: how he rejected the divine mission, how he deserted God. Again, other sailors might have punished him for endangering their lives, but these do not. Even now, they are not against him, nor do they consider the possibility of getting rid of him. After his confession, they go back to work, trying to guide the ship out of the danger zone. The idea of throwing Jonah into the sea is not theirs, it is his. At first, they refuse to hear of it. True, he is a stranger, and responsible for their troubles and maybe for their deaths, but they try to dissuade him from seeking a solution in death. How can we not admire such generosity of spirit, such refinement in people who have a reputation of being tough guys?

As for the sea? Not guilty, not even of maliciousness. As God's instrument, it knows its limitations. Its function is to remind Jonah of his duties as man and emissary of God. The sea cannot disobey—as the wind cannot. As soon as Jonah leaves the boat, the sea quiets down. The sea bears no grudge, not against the sailors, not even against Jonah. The sea does what it must because the wind forces it. Nor does the wind have a choice: it was created for that purpose.

The same reasoning applies to the whale. The whale swallows the suicidal prophet but it also saves him; it could stifle him; it does not. It could keep him prisoner longer; instead it sets him ashore safe and sound.

As for God, He has rarely shown Himself to be as just and as charitable. He readily consents to humiliate His own spokesman in order to spare Nineveh, the sinful city. If He is cruel towards Jonah, it is for his own good; so as to teach him the importance of repentance, to show him the way to humanity rather than to abstract absolutes. He teaches Jonah not how to suffer but how to remain humble in the face of suffering. Justice must be human, truth must be human, compassion must be human. The way to God leads through man, however alien, however sinful he may be. Naturally, Jonah has every right in the world to be angry with God—but we do not. The rest of us should be grateful to God, who, like a father, may threaten His wayward children but shies away from executing His threats. So then, in this story we should view God as being good and merciful with all His children, Jonah included. Though he has to go through fear and pain, that is a small price to pay for saving first an entire shipload of people and then an entire city.

But who then is the villain? Despite our earlier portayal of him as angry, selfish, and indifferent, Jonah in fact chooses to take refuge in sleep because he is too sensitive to other people's pain, too open to their suffering. He finds it so unbearable that he tries to escape. Because he knows the horrors of reality, he runs away. A kind and gracious prophet, a friend and defender of man, Jonah is aware of his own helplessness when faced with human misery. If he refuses to go to Nineveh, it is not because he wants it destroyed. Quite the contrary: he does not want to deliver the threat. It is as if he told God: "I do not agree with Your way of ruling Your world! You say to man: be just or perish. Don't You know that this choice is inhuman? You who know everything, don't You see that life is mixture and synthesis, and not polarization? That to be human means to sin a bit and then repent, and then sin again and repent again, and start all over again from the beginning? Why do You condemn Nineveh to total extinction?" Jonah shuns Nineveh because of his enormous love for humanity.

At that point in his life, Jonah deserves our love and affection. Think about him in Nineveh—a stranger among strangers, roaming the streets and marketplaces, urged on by a mysterious impulse, shouting again and again five or six words, always the same: "In forty days, Nineveh will be destroyed."

There he is, the man who knows, the man who sees the future, and yet Jonah makes no speeches, writes no poems, composes no litany. He goes on repeating five, six words, always the same. He knows that when the life of a community is in peril, one may not indulge in philosophy or art. At that moment his anguish is even greater than it was while in the belly of the whale. His own death does not frighten him; the death of others does.

Yes, Jonah acts as spokesman for mankind in general. A true prophet, he is faithful to tradition and wishes to serve not only as God's messenger to mankind and Israel, but also as man's and Israel's messenger to God. When forced to choose between God and Israel, he chooses Israel—even if that means he will be punished. He will not do harm to Israel, even if ordered to do so by God Himself.

His strange and passionate behavior reveals his

lucid devotion and commitment to his people: though he is a prophet—and must speak words not his own—he refuses to testify, to uncover the truth if that truth is likely to damage the reputation and security of his people. The nation of Israel is in danger—it has always been in danger—and Jonah feels it is not the right moment to critize its policies, to judge its decisions, for doing so would retroactively justify the hostility it arouses among other nations.

At that point, how can one not empathize with Jonah, the brave and magnificent prophet who flees abroad but whose heart remains with his people?

What does the story mean? What does it teach? Why must Jews repeat it year after year during Yom Kippur services?

Two hypotheses, two major themes:

One: the emphasis is on repentance, which has dominated Jewish thought from its origins, since Adam and Cain. Unlike Greek mythology, Judaism rejects the concept of fatalism. Fate is not inexorable, decisions are never irrevocable. Man is not a toy whose functioning is prearranged; his link to infinity assures him access to endless possibilities. Destiny's march can be stopped; its triumph is not predetermined. In other words, the cycle of crime and punishment can be halted before it is completed. Evil can be aborted, diverted, vanquished. Better yet, it can be transformed; it can undergo endless mutations—by choosing repentance. It is sufficient for man to take hold of himself, to say to himself: "Enough—I must turn around before it's too late," and all evil decrees will be lifted. Such is the theme and the teaching of the Book of Jonah.

Teshuva means an act of consciousness, of awareness, of willingness to take sides and responsibility for the future. One cannot modify the past, but one is given the power to shape the future. It all depends on individuals and the community; they can, if they wish, foil destiny and celebrate free choice. The lesson in Jonah is that nothing is written, nothing is sealed: God's will itself may change. Even though punishment has been programmed, it may be cancelled. Therein lies the beauty and the grandeur of Jewish tradition: every human being is granted one more chance, one more opportunity to start his life all over again. Just as God has the power to begin, man has the power to continue by beginning again—and again.

The second theme is the universality of the Jewish message. Jonah is not the only prophet who, in the name of God, speaks to other nations; others did so before him. But Jonah is the only one whose mission is to serve other nations exclusively. "Go to Nineveh," says God. Only to Nineveh—not to Jerusalem. Not even to Jaffa; he sails to Tarshish . . . from Jaffa.

Jonah's task is to bring God's word to the Gentiles—without forsaking his own people, his own memories and beliefs. In other words, he is to teach the Gentiles without ceasing to be Jewish. More than that, it is the Jew in him who will teach the Gentiles. The more Jewish the poet, the more universal his message. The more Jewish his soul, the more human his concerns A Jew who does not feel for his Jews, who does not share in their sorrows and joys, cannot feel for other people. And a Jew who is concerned with his fellow Jews is inevitably concerned with the fate of other people as well.

Remember the dialogue Jonah has with the sailors when they ask him: "Who are you? What are you doing?" He answers: "I am Jewish and I fear God, who has created heaven and earth." That is all, that is enough. Without the slightest hesitation, he reveals his Jewish identity to them. He does not hide under disguises and false pretenses. *Ivri anokhi*, he says. "I am Jewish. And it is as a Jew that I am telling you that God is to be feared."

There is a certain amount of humor in this exchange: the sailors ask Jonah what he does, and he tells them who he is. Still, Jonah is right. To be Jewish means to do things, to speak up and take a stand. Heine was wrong: to be Jewish is not a calamity. It is not even a problem. It is a philosophy of action.

As a Jew, Jonah feels gifted and strong enough to confront the world and influence its future. As a Jew, he feels he has certain things to tell the nations of the earth. As a Jew, he feels he has both the right and the duty to say: "If you do not change, if Nineveh does not stop hating Jerusalem, its hate will spread beyond its borders and the world of Nineveh will lie in ruins."

We understand Jonah in contemporary terms. He knows that men are evil; he knows they deserve punishment; he also knows that God is capable of inflicting it. Nineveh has done much harm to Israel; Jonah the Jew might have wished to serve as an emissary of vengeance and retribution. But, paradoxically, Jonah the Jew ultimately saves Nineveh, just as our generation may be called upon to save a world filled with guilt. There are those of us who feel that only by remembering what it has done to the Jewish people can the world be spared from bringing the catastrophe upon itself.

Jonah thus emerges as an unparalleled humanist and pacifist. Beaten by life, humbled by God, this anti-hero, though he chooses despair for himself and others, thinks of others before he thinks of himself. He opts for life, however filled with anguish, in order to prevent others from dying.

When all is said and done, the real hero of the story is a small insignificant plant; the Kikayon is both the hero of the story and its victim. Brought into the world only to die, only to serve as an example with its quick death, the plant appears and vanishes. It dies so as to bring light and life to a distant city named Nineveh.

God feels no pity for the plant; only Jonah does, though we learn it indirectly. Jonah does not say it; God does, and we must believe Him, mustn't we? Jonah is deeply moving. He who has seen so much suffering in the world and who anticipates even more, weeps over a little plant, which has given him protection.

A man who feels such compassion for a plant cannot be insensitive to people. Jonah's problem is that he is too sensitive. He does not wish Nineveh to die, yet he does not wish Nineveh to live at the expense of Israel. To love mankind is honorable; to love it against Israel is not. Is that the reason for Jonah's death wish? Does he wish to die because of the inner moral conflict of reconciling his love of man with his incommensurate love for his people? Does God show him the tragic fate of the plant to provide the ultimate illustration that all things are related, that one must feel pity for both Nineveh and the Kikayon, that one must love other people through one's own—and never outside one's own?

Of course, on a practical level, and viewed in the light of today's events, all this is neither easy nor simple. So what then? Who ever said that the quest for truth must and can be simple? The Book of Jonah offers proof that nothing is ever simple. All its characters stumble over obstacle after obstacle, yet they continue to search, to love, to live, to remember. All have a mission—and ultimately, they fulfill it.

The most touching aspect of the book is its ending, or rather, its lack of ending. God points to the dead plant and asks Jonah the famous and unfair question: "You feel sorry for the plant and you want Me not to feel sorry for Nineveh and its people and its animals?" Thus we learn that Jonah *did* feel pity for the Kikayon.

If indeed Jonah answered God's question, the answer has not been recorded. The book ends with God's word, which is only natural: God makes sure He has the last word, always. But, uniquely, the book ends on a question—and that is what leaves us astonished and deeply affected. How many other sacred and eternal, inspired and inspiring books are there in which the last sentence is neither affirmation nor injunction, nor even a statement, but, quite simply, a question?

SOURCES:

Mishna
Talmud Bavli
Talmud Yerushalmi
Midrash Rabba
Midrash Tankhuma
Midrash Eikha
Legends of the Bible by Louis Ginzburg
Jérémie by André Neher
L'Essence du Prophétisme by André Neher
L'Exil de la Parole by André Neher
Moses by David Daiches
Essays in Jewish Thought by Nahum N. Glatzer
The Sages—Their Concepts and Beliefs by E. E. Urbach

Five Biblical Portraits is based on lectures delivered at Boston University and the 92nd Street "Y" in New York. This volume is part of a series that began with *Messengers of God*.